HOW TO WRITE FANTASY : THE ULTIMATE GUIDE TO CREATING UNFORGETTABLE ADVENTURES

AURNY AIRDUVAL

HOW TO WRITE FANTASY :
THE ULTIMATE GUIDE TO CREATING UNFORGETTABLE ADVENTURES

This work, including images, is protected in all its components by the provisions of the Copyright Law, particularly those relating to copyright. Any reproduction or distribution to third parties, whether free of charge or for a fee, of all or part of this work, is strictly prohibited and constitutes infringement.

Copyright © 2023 – All rights reserved

Aurny AIRDUVAL

Foreword

Welcome to the captivating world of fantasy writing, a realm where imagination reigns supreme, and extraordinary worlds come to life through words. As a fantasy author, I will guide you through the intricacies of this epic literary genre, sharing valuable insights for crafting unforgettable adventures.

Fantasy is more than just a literary genre; it is a gateway to the unknown, a passage to magical realms and parallel realities where possibilities are endless. As a writer, fantasy provides you with the opportunity to push the boundaries of your creativity, to conceive extraordinary worlds, creatures, and powers, and to explore profound themes while offering an escape to your readers.

1. The pillars of fantasy

Fantasy is characterized by elements that are unique to the genre, setting it apart from other literary forms. Whether you're a seasoned fantasy author or a budding writer, you are well acquainted with these foundational principles:

Imaginary world: at the heart of every fantasy tale lies a fictional world, a canvas upon which you paint enchanting landscapes, unique cultures, and extraordinary civilizations.

Magic: magic is the lifeblood of fantasy. It can be structured with strict rules or shrouded in mystery, but it always serves as a source of wonder and amazement.

Fantastic creatures: mythical beings, from majestic dragons to mysterious elves, populate the fantastical realms where the action unfolds.

Heroism: heroes, with their epic quests and extraordinary destinies, stand as pillars of fantasy.

Archetypes: classic archetypes, from the chosen one to the wise mentor, guide characters and narratives along familiar paths.

2. Why write fantasy

As a fantasy author, you are the creator of worlds, the storyteller of epics, and the keeper of the secrets of imagination. Your pen unveils tales filled with courage, discovery, and wonders. You transpose real-world issues into fantastical contexts, providing readers with a magical mirror to reflect on their own lives.

Fantasy allows you to connect with an audience that shares your passion for the unexplored, the intriguing, and the mystical. Fantasy readers are hungry for discoveries, thirsty for quests, and ready to be enchanted. By writing fantasy, you have the privilege of leading them into extraordinary realms and forming lasting bonds with them.

Part 1

Introduction to fantasy

Chapter 1

The essential elements of fantasy

Fantasy possesses unique characteristics that set this literary genre apart from others. We will delve deeply into these essential elements, exploring how to harness them to craft captivating worlds and unforgettable narratives.

1. Imaginary world

One of the fundamental elements of fantasy is the creation of an imaginary world. It is within these fictional realms that your stories come to life, and as a fantasy author, you are the master of the universe you create. Every detail, from geography to culture, must be carefully crafted to immerse readers in your alternate reality.

Fantasy worlds can vary significantly, from magical medieval realms to exotic extraterrestrial planets. You have complete freedom to design the backdrop of your narrative, but ensure that this world is both coherent and detailed. Fantasy readers appreciate authenticity and immersion.

2. Magic

Magic is another indispensable pillar of fantasy. It can be the heart of your universe, introducing supernatural elements to your story. Magic can be structured with specific rules, elaborate systems, and limitations, or it can be more mysterious, residing in the dark corners of your world.

Creating a unique magic system is an opportunity to showcase your creativity. Consider how magic operates in your world, how it is wielded, its costs, and consequences. Magic can be a benevolent or destructive force, playing a pivotal role in the narrative arc of your story.

3. Fantastic creatures

Fantastic creatures are another distinctive feature of fantasy. From majestic dragons to mysterious elves, trolls, dwarves, and many others, these mythical beings populate the fantastical worlds you create. You can bring these creatures to life in a way that makes them memorable and meaningful to your narrative.

When introducing fantastic creatures into your story, consider their role in the plot. How do they interact with the main characters? Do they have unique characteristics that set them apart? By making these creatures integral elements of your world, you enhance the immersion for your readers.

4. The heroic quest

The heroic quest is a classic narrative pattern in fantasy. In many fantasy tales, a central character embarks on a perilous journey to achieve a significant goal. This journey can take various forms, whether it's destroying an evil artifact, saving a kingdom in distress, or uncovering one's true destiny.

As an author, the heroic quest provides a solid narrative structure for your story. It creates tension, challenges, and opportunities for character growth. Readers are drawn to epic journeys and triumphs over adversity, making it an essential element of fantasy.

5. Archetypes

Archetypes are recurring characters and motifs in fantasy. You can use these archetypes as powerful narrative tools. Classic archetypes include the chosen one, the wise mentor, the formidable villain, and others.

Thoughtful use of archetypes can help guide the story's progression and establish emotional connections with readers. However, remember that subverting classic archetypes can also be an effective way to surprise readers and create more nuanced characters.

The essential elements of fantasy are the cornerstones of this captivating genre. Mastering these elements is crucial for crafting immersive worlds, powerful narratives, and unforgettable characters.

Chapter 2

The evolution of fantasy and its subgenres

We will explore the roots of fantasy, its key developments over time, as well as the numerous subgenres that have emerged to enrich the landscape of fantasy.

1. The origins of fantasy

As a literary genre, fantasy draws its roots from ancient tales, legends, and mythologies from cultures around the world. Epic narratives such as "The Epic of Gilgamesh" and "The Iliad and The Odyssey" significantly influenced the development of fantasy. Stories of heroes, monsters, and magic were at the core of these tales.

Over the centuries, fantasy has also been shaped by works like J.R.R. Tolkien's "The Lord of the Rings," C.S. Lewis's "The Chronicles of Narnia," and Robert E. Howard's "Conan the Barbarian," which have played a key role in defining the genre in its modern form.

2. The golden age of fantasy

The period of the Golden Age of Fantasy, spanning from the 1930s to the 1950s, witnessed the publication of some of the genre's most iconic works. It was during this time that J.R.R. Tolkien released "The Lord of the Rings," thereby establishing many conventions of modern fantasy. Authors such as C.S. Lewis, Fritz Leiber, and Michael Moorcock also made significant contributions to the flourishing of fantasy.

3. Contemporary fantasy

Contemporary fantasy is a genre in constant evolution. Over the past few decades, new authors have brought fresh and innovative perspectives to fantasy. Notable works include J.K. Rowling's "Harry Potter," George R.R. Martin's "A Song of Ice and Fire," and Robert Jordan's "The Wheel of Time." These authors have expanded the spectrum of fantasy by introducing new themes, darker plots, and complex characters.

4. The subgenres of fantasy

Fantasy is a vast genre, and over time, numerous subgenres have emerged to explore specific themes. Here are some of the most common subgenres of fantasy:

High fantasy: this subgenre is characterized by elaborate worlds, epic quests, and a struggle between good and evil. Works by J.R.R. Tolkien and C.S. Lewis are iconic examples of high fantasy.

Low fantasy: in contrast to high fantasy, low fantasy unfolds in worlds closer to reality, where magic is less pervasive. J.K. Rowling's "Harry Potter" is an example of low fantasy.

Dark fantasy: dark fantasy explores dark themes, often featuring morally ambiguous heroes and complex situations. Works by George R.R. Martin exemplify dark fantasy.

Sword and sorcery: this subgenre emphasizes individual adventures, battles, and conquests. The stories of Robert E. Howard's Conan the Barbarian embody sword and sorcery.

Urban fantasy: urban fantasy transposes fantastical elements into contemporary urban environments. Cassandra Clare's "The Mortal Instruments" series is an example of urban fantasy.

The history of fantasy is rich and varied. It reflects the aspirations, dreams, and obsessions of humanity throughout the ages. Understanding the history of fantasy and the various subgenres that comprise it provides valuable perspective for shaping your own work.

Part 2

Planning and preparation

Chapter 3

Finding inspiration for your fantasy world

The creation of a unique imaginary universe is one of the most exhilarating aspects of writing a fantasy book. But how do you find inspiration for a world that will captivate your readers? We will explore strategies and sources of inspiration to bring a captivating fantasy world to life.

1. Inspiration sources

Inspiration for a fantasy universe can come from various sources. It's essential to keep an open mind and remain attentive to the ideas around you. Here are some sources of inspiration for fantasy:

Mythology and legends: myths and legends from around the world abound with creatures, gods, heroes, and narratives that can serve as a foundation for your own fantasy world.

Nature: nature, with its diverse landscapes, wildlife, and flora, can be an endless source of inspiration. From enchanted forests to towering mountains, nature can shape the geography of your world.

History: real-world history, with its epochs, conflicts, and advancements, can provide elements to create civilizations, cultures, and conflicts in your fantasy universe.

Dreams and imagination: your own dreams and imagination can be powerful sources of inspiration. Let yourself be carried away by imaginary scenarios and ideas that arise from your mind.

Travel: exploring the real world, visiting new places, encountering different cultures, and observing diverse landscapes can help enrich your understanding of the world's diversity, which can be valuable for creating your own fantasy universe.

2. Building your world

When you begin constructing your fantasy universe, consider the following questions:

What is the geography of your world? Create maps, continents, regions, seas, and mountains to bring your world to life.

What cultures and civilizations populate your world? Explore the customs, languages, beliefs, and lifestyles of these peoples.

What are the magic systems and specific rules governing your universe? Define how magic operates, what types of magic exist, and if there are costs associated with its use.

What fantastic creatures inhabit your world? Invent unique creatures, mythical animals, and fantastical races to enrich your universe.

What conflicts, quests, and stakes are at the heart of your story? Identify the challenges your characters must overcome and the goals they pursue.

3. Subverting expectations

Subverting expectations is a powerful technique in fantasy. When you find your inspiration, consider how you can take familiar elements and twist them in unexpected ways. This can surprise readers and make your fantasy world even more captivating.

Finding inspiration for your fantasy universe is the first step towards creating an unforgettable story. Sources of inspiration are all around you, whether from ancient myths, majestic nature, or your own dreams. As you begin to build your world, make sure to breathe life into unique cultures, geographies, magic systems, and characters that will enchant and astonish your readers. The process of creating a fantasy universe is an adventure in itself, and there is no limit to what you can imagine.

Chapter 4

Creating your world: geography, history, and culture

Creating the universe of your fantasy is a crucial step to immerse your readers in a memorable experience. We will explore how to bring to life the geography, history, and culture of your fantastical world.

1. The geography of your world

The geography of your world plays a major role in creating an immersive atmosphere. Consider the following elements when designing the geography of your universe:

Mapping: create detailed maps of your world, including continents, seas, mountains, and forests. Maps are essential tools for both you and your readers.

Climate: define the climates of different regions in your world. Climates influence the fauna, flora, and culture of each area.

Landmarks: identify important landmarks, such as cities, sacred mountains, enchanted lakes, that will play a key role in your story.

Natural resources: consider the natural resources available in your world, such as rare minerals, magical plants, or sources of power.

Unique regions: create unique regions with special features. For example, an ancient forest housing spirits or a desert haunted by legendary creatures.

2. The history of your world

The history of your world is the accumulation of stories, myths, and conflicts that have shaped its past. Consider these elements to enrich the history of your universe:

Myths and legends: create myths and legends that explain the origin of your world, its gods, heroes, and foes.

Ancient history: explore the past epochs of your world, highlighting significant events that have influenced its present.

Wars and conflicts: identify wars, conflicts, and alliances that have forged the political history of your universe.

Historical figures: introduce legendary historical figures who have left their mark on your world.

Artifacts and relics: imagine magical objects, artifacts, and relics that hold historical and spiritual significance.

3. The culture of your world

The culture of your world serves as the backdrop for your characters and their actions. To create a rich and authentic culture, consider these aspects:

Languages: develop fictional languages for the different cultures of your world. Think about how these languages can reflect the history and geography.

Customs and traditions: identify customs, traditions, and rituals that define each culture. How do they celebrate weddings, funerals, or other significant events?

Social hierarchy: explore the structure of society, including social classes, governments, and power systems.

Religion: create divine pantheons, religious beliefs, and places of worship that play a role in the lives of your characters.

Arts and crafts: identify forms of art, craftsmanship, and entertainment that are typical of each culture.

4. Consistency and credibility

Consistency is essential to maintain the credibility of your fantasy universe. Ensure that all the elements you create, whether it's geography, history, or culture, logically fit into the world you've envisioned. Consistent details contribute to making your universe believable to readers.

The creation of the geography, history, and culture of your fantastical world is an act of creativity and imagination. Your universe should be rich, authentic, and captivating so that readers willingly immerse themselves in it. As you build your world, don't forget to explore the nuances, conflicts, and interactions between the different elements of your universe.

Chapter 5

Creating a magic system

Magic is a fundamental element of fantasy, offering endless possibilities to create extraordinary worlds. We will explore how to create a coherent and compelling magic system for your universe.

1 Defining the rules of magic

When creating a magic system, it is essential to establish clear rules for its functioning. This maintains consistency in your narrative and prevents magic from becoming an easy problem-solving device. You should consider the following elements:

Origin of magic: explore the origin of magic in your fantastical world. Is it tied to gods, nature, artifacts, or other sources? Understanding this origin can impact how characters interact with magic.

Limits and constraints: every magic system must have limits and constraints. For example, magic might be draining for users, have undesirable side effects, or be subject to strict laws.

Cost of magic: determine the cost of using magic. Can users sacrifice something in exchange for their power, such as life force, memories, or even mental health?

Learning and training: characters who use magic should require training or apprenticeship to master their power. This can introduce initiation quests or master magicians.

2. Types of magic

There are numerous types of magic in fantasy. Here are some of the most common:

Elemental magic: magic related to natural elements such as fire, water, earth, and air.

Dark magic: magic associated with dark forces, often linked to necromancy or black magic.

Divine magic: magic granted by gods or divine entities, commonly used by priests or paladins.

Enchantment magic: magic related to the modification of objects or living beings.

Time magic: the ability to manipulate time, such as divination or time travel.

Rune magic: the use of magical symbols to create spells or enchantments.

3. Consequences of magic

Magic should have consequences in your imaginary world. The effects of magic can be positive or negative, but they should impact the plot and characters. You should consider the following elements:

Side effects: magical spells may have unexpected or undesirable side effects.

Power imbalance: magic can create an imbalance of power between magic users and non-users. This can be a source of conflict.

Forbidden magic: some types of magic may be forbidden or taboo, creating moral stakes.

4. Using magic in the plot

Magic can play a key role in the plot of your narrative. It can be used to solve problems, create obstacles, or reinforce the themes of the story.

By developing a coherent magic system, integrating magic meaningfully into the plot, and maintaining consistency throughout your narrative, you can create a memorable reading experience for your audience. Magic is an exciting element of fantasy, and its creation and usage require careful planning to enrich your imaginary world.

Part 3

Memorable characters

Chapter 6

Creating fantasy characters

Characters are the soul of your fantasy story. Whether they are brave heroes, ambiguous anti-heroes, or formidable antagonists, creating rich and memorable characters is essential to captivate your readers. We will explore the design of these three key character types.

1. The heroes of your story

The heroes are the protagonists of your narrative, the main characters that readers follow and become attached to. Here are some elements to consider when creating fantastic heroes:

Motivations: determine the deep motivations of your hero. What drives them to act? Is it a desire for justice, a call to adventure, or a personal goal?

Strengths and weaknesses: give your hero distinctive strengths, but don't forget to give them weaknesses too. Flawed characters are more nuanced and realistic.

Evolution: plan the growth and development of your hero throughout the story. The challenges they face should contribute to their evolution.

Relationships: create meaningful relationships between your hero and other characters. Interactions with allies, mentors, or friends can enrich your character.

Obstacles: introduce obstacles and conflicts that your hero must overcome to achieve their goal. These challenges can include adversaries, puzzles, or moral dilemmas.

2. The ambiguous anti-heroes

Anti-heroes are complex characters whose motivations and actions are not necessarily morally pure. They often grapple with internal conflicts and are more nuanced than traditional heroes. Here are some considerations for creating anti-heroes:

Ambiguous morality: anti-heroes can be morally ambiguous, sometimes acting selfishly or amorally, but they may also have moments of bravery or redemption.

Uncertain motivations: explore the contradictory motivations of your anti-hero. They might be driven by revenge, survival, or other complex motives.

Moral compromises: anti-heroes are often faced with moral dilemmas where they must choose between two evils. These tough choices add depth to their personality.

Gradual evolution: anti-heroes may evolve slowly towards a more positive alignment over the course of the story, or they may remain tormented souls until the end.

3. Memorable antagonists

Antagonists are the forces that oppose the heroes and drive the conflict in the story. Here's how to create memorable antagonists in fantasy:

Justifiable motivations: the best antagonists have motivations that are, at least partially, understandable. Explain why they act the way they do.

Complexity: avoid creating one-dimensional antagonists. Give them distinctive character traits, weaknesses, and personal histories.

Relationships: antagonists can have relationships with other characters, whether as rivals, allies, or enemies. These relationships add depth to their personality.

Formidable obstacles: provide your antagonists with powers, skills, or resources that make them formidable adversaries for the heroes.

Negative evolution or redemption: some antagonists may evolve negatively throughout the story, while others may be inclined towards redemption.

4. Subverting expectations

Subverting expectations can be a powerful way to surprise readers with your characters. For example, an anti-hero may exhibit unexpected heroic qualities, or an antagonist may reveal more nuanced aspects of their personality.

Creating memorable heroes, anti-heroes, and antagonists is a crucial step in bringing your fantasy story to life. Each character should be complex, motivated, and undergo development. The relationships between characters, moral conflicts, and obstacles contribute to making your narrative engaging. As you explore these character archetypes, don't forget to add unique elements that set them apart from stereotypes.

Chapter 7

The evolution of your characters

The evolution of characters is an essential component of any good fantasy story. Readers want to follow characters who grow, change, and overcome challenges. We will explore how to plan and execute character development convincingly.

1. The foundations of character evolution

The foundations of character evolution involve showcasing how heroes, anti-heroes, and even antagonists change throughout the story. Here are some fundamental points to keep in mind:

Goals and motivations: characters evolve by pursuing goals and motivations that drive them to change and grow.

Conflicts and challenges: obstacles, conflicts, and challenges characters face act as catalysts for their evolution. These trials push them to change.

Relationships: interactions with other characters can influence character evolution. Friendships, romances, mentors, and enemies all play a role.

Decisions and consequences: the choices characters make and the consequences of those choices are essential to their development. The repercussions of their actions shape their journey.

2. Character arc

The character arc is the trajectory a character follows throughout the story. It can involve a positive transformation (from ignorance to wisdom) or a negative one (from innocence to corruption). Here are some common types of character arcs:

Hero's journey arc: the character moves from the ordinary to the heroic. They learn to overcome their fears and stand against evil.

Redemption arc: an immoral or bad character seeks redemption by performing positive actions to offset their past.

Self-discovery arc: the character learns more about themselves, overcomes doubts and uncertainties, and finds their true identity.

Corruption arc: the character starts as a hero or honorable individual but is corrupted by dark forces or choices.

Sacrifice arc: the character sacrifices something precious for the common good, leading to personal growth.

3. Avoiding too sudden developments

Character development should be believable and gradual. Avoid abrupt transformations that seem artificial. Characters should face obstacles and dilemmas that naturally push them towards change.

4. Emotions and growth

Emotions play a major role in character development. Moments of sadness, joy, anger, and fear can all be catalysts for change. Readers should feel the emotional evolution of the characters throughout the story.

5. The evolution of antagonists

The evolution of antagonists is just as crucial as that of protagonists. Villains with complex motivations and well-developed character arcs are often more memorable. Some antagonists may evolve towards redemption, while others may become more malevolent.

Character evolution is a fundamental element of fantasy storytelling. Readers want to see characters grow, change, and overcome challenges. By understanding the motivations, conflicts, and relationships of your characters, you can create compelling character arcs that will captivate your audience's imagination.

Chapter 8

The psychology of characters

The psychology of characters is an essential element to make your heroes, anti-heroes, and antagonists deep and convincing. We will explore the aspects of character psychology and how to integrate them into your imaginary story.

1. Psychological complexity

Creating psychologically complex characters involves giving them thoughts, emotions, and motivations that make them realistic. Here are elements to consider when developing the psychology of your characters:

Deep motivations: understand the inner motivations of your characters. What drives them to act? Is it the quest for truth, revenge, or the pursuit of happiness?

Strengths and weaknesses: every character should have strengths and weaknesses. Explore their fears, doubts, and vulnerabilities, in addition to their skills and strengths.

Traumas and wounds: past experiences can have a significant impact on a character's psychology. Develop the traumas or emotional wounds that have shaped who they are.

Internal conflicts: internal conflicts are a rich source of complexity. Characters may be torn between conflicting duties, divergent loyalties, or opposing desires.

Emotional evolution: show how the emotions of your characters evolve throughout the story. Feelings of anger, sadness, joy, and fear should reflect the experiences they undergo.

2. Moral dilemmas

Moral dilemmas are situations where characters face difficult choices, often between right and wrong or conflicting values. These dilemmas allow for a deep exploration of the characters' psychology. For example, a hero may be faced with the decision to save one life at the expense of many others, or an anti-hero may have to choose between loyalty to friends and the pursuit of personal goals.

3. The psychology of antagonists

Antagonists can also benefit from in-depth psychological exploration. Understanding the motivations and justifications for their actions can add nuance to their personality. The best antagonists are those that readers can comprehend, even if they don't agree with them.

4. Psychological evolution

Psychological evolution is the internal transformation that characters undergo throughout the story. Their psychology must evolve in response to the events and challenges they face. Characters can become stronger, wiser, more resilient, or conversely, more bitter, more cynical, or more desperate.

5. Portraying psychology through actions and dialogue

Character psychology can be expressed through their actions and dialogue. Show how they react to adversity, discuss their fears or dreams, and interact with other characters.

The psychology of fantastical characters is a crucial component in creating a memorable story. Psychologically complex and nuanced characters allow readers to identify with them, become attached to their fate, and experience the story through their eyes. By developing the motivations, internal conflicts, and emotions of your characters, you can add depth to your fantastical narrative.

Part 4

Narrative structure

Chapter 9

The basic structure

A good narrative structure is essential to maintain the readers' interest and create a captivating story. We present a basic structure, highlighting its key elements. You can draw inspiration from this framework to shape your story or customize it according to your preferences.

Act 1: Introduction and establishment of the universe

1. Introduction of the fantastic world

Quickly present the fantastic world, its rules of magic, unique creatures, and distinctive elements.

Establish the atmosphere, mood, and aesthetics of the fantastic universe.

2. Introduction of characters

Introduce the main characters, including the hero, anti-hero, allies, and antagonists.

Show their motivations, personalities, and initial conflicts.

3. Initial conflict

Present an initial conflict or problem that drives the plot. This can be the starting point of the hero's quest or journey.

4. The call to adventure

The hero is usually prompted to undertake a journey or quest that leads them into the unknown.

The call to adventure may be linked to a prophecy, an imminent threat, or an extraordinary opportunity.

Act 2: Plot development

5. Journey And adventure

The hero embarks on their journey or quest, discovers new places, meets key characters, and overcomes obstacles.

6. Conflicts and obstacles

The hero faces escalating challenges, including magical trials, powerful enemies, and moral dilemmas.

7. Revelation of magic

Further explore the magic system of your world and show how it impacts the plot.

Characters may learn new magical skills or confront magical artifacts.

8. Character evolution

Characters evolve in response to events and conflicts. Their motivations, alliances, and psychologies undergo changes

Act 3: Climax and resolution

9. Final confrontation
Protagonists face the main antagonist or ultimate threat.
The final confrontation is a moment of high tension, epic battle, or resolution of conflicts.

10. Plot resolution
Major plot questions find their answers, whether it's defeating the antagonist, achieving the quest, or discovering the truth.

11. Epilogue
Give readers a glimpse of what happens to the characters after the plot resolution.
Conclude the story with a satisfying closing note.

This basic structure follows a familiar pattern but offers ample room for creativity and originality. By adhering to this structure, you can create a coherent, engaging, and immersive story. However, remember that narrative structure is just one part of the equation. Character psychology, writing style, and world-building also play a key role in crafting a memorable story.

Chapter 10

Quests and the chosen one's journey

Quests are an iconic element of fantasy, and the concept of the chosen one embarking on an extraordinary journey is a common narrative structure. We will delve into the essential elements of quests in fantasy and how to create a memorable journey for the chosen one in your story.

1. The quest of the chosen one

The chosen one character is often the main protagonist in a fantasy story. They are destined to accomplish an extraordinary task or defeat an imminent threat. Here are the key elements of the chosen one's quest:

The prophecy: the chosen one's quest is typically associated with an ancient prophecy or prediction that foretells the arrival of a specific hero.

The epic task: the chosen one is entrusted with a monumental task, often related to the world's survival, restoring balance, or defeating a great menace.

The initiatory journey: the quest serves as an initiatory journey for the chosen one, allowing them to grow, learn, and evolve throughout the story.

Allies and obstacles: the chosen one is usually joined by a group of allies, each bringing specific skills and knowledge. However, they must also face powerful obstacles, including formidable enemies and magical trials.

2. The hero's journey

The journey of the chosen one often follows the structure of the "Hero's Journey," a classic narrative pattern developed by Joseph Campbell. This journey consists of several stages, including:

The call to adventure: the chosen one receives a call to adventure that urges them to leave their comfort zone.

The refusal of the call: initially, the chosen one may hesitate or refuse the call to adventure due to fear, uncertainty, or other obstacles.

Meeting the mentor: the chosen one often encounters a mentor or guide who provides advice, knowledge, and essential tools for their quest.

Trials and allies: the chosen one faces a series of trials, gains allies, and acquires experience throughout their journey.

The ordainment of the quest: the chosen one approaches the final goal of their quest and must make crucial choices to achieve it.

The final confrontation: the chosen one confronts the main antagonist or the ultimate threat and must overcome this confrontation to succeed in their quest.

The transformed return: after completing their task, the chosen one returns to the ordinary world, transformed by their journey.

3. Subversion of expectations

While the chosen one's quest pattern is classic in fantasy, there are many opportunities for subverting expectations. You can surprise readers by altering certain stages of the journey, questioning the prophecy, or exploring the unexpected consequences of the chosen one's actions.

Quests in fantasy, especially those of the chosen one, are an essential element of narrative structure. They provide a powerful framework for telling epic stories, exploring themes of destiny and courage, and evolving characters. However, originality lies in how you personalize this structure, adding unique elements and subverting reader expectations.

Chapter 11

Secondary plots and subtexts

Secondary plots and subtexts are crucial elements to enrich your story. They allow for further development of the world, characters, and themes of the narrative. We will explore how to skillfully integrate secondary plots and subtexts to add depth to your storytelling.

1. The benefits of secondary plots

Secondary plots bring several advantages to your story:

Character development: they allow for a deeper exploration of characters by showing other aspects of their lives, relationships, and motivations.

World enrichment: they expand the fantasy world by exploring places, cultures, and magical elements that are not directly tied to the main plot.

Themes and symbolism: secondary plots can be used to delve into deeper themes, metaphors, and symbols.

Suspense and tension: they create suspense by maintaining the reader's interest, giving the impression that the story is complex and ever-evolving.

2. Creating compelling secondary plots

To craft compelling secondary plots, follow these steps:

Objective and significance: each secondary plot should have a clear objective and significance. Why is it important to the story? How does it contribute to the characters or the universe?

Relation to the main plot: secondary plots should not be entirely disconnected from the main plot. They can be linked through themes, consequences, or common characters.

Characters in action: involve the main characters in the secondary plot. Readers should become attached to these characters and care about their fate.

Revelations and connections: secondary plots can unveil key information about the main plot, clues, or contextual elements that become important later on.

Conflicts and obstacles: like in the main plot, secondary plots should feature challenges, dilemmas, and conflicts to maintain interest.

3. Subtexts

Subtexts are the implicit elements of the story that are often inferred by readers. They can involve emotions, characters' secret motivations, hidden themes, or unspoken tensions. Here's how to integrate them:

Dialogues and actions: subtexts can be suggested through dialogues, characters' emotional reactions, and their actions.

Ambiguity: don't explicitly reveal everything. Leave clues for readers to draw their own conclusions.

Deep themes: subtexts can be used to explore deeper themes in fantasy, such as power, morality, or the nature of reality.

Character evolution: subtexts can reveal the emotional and psychological developments of characters.

4. The subversion of expectations

The skillful use of subplots and subtexts can also serve to subvert the reader's expectations. You can lead them down a false trail to surprise them later in the story.

Subplots and subtexts are powerful tools to enrich your story. They add depth, realism, and interest to your narrative by further developing characters, the world, and themes. However, balance is crucial: make sure these elements contribute to the overall story without overwhelming it with unnecessary information.

Part 5

Writing and style

Chapter 12

The writing style in fantasy

The writing style is a crucial element to immerse readers in the fantastical universe you've created. We'll explore how to use writing style to craft a magical, captivating, and immersive atmosphere in your fantasy narrative.

1. Using descriptions

Descriptions play a crucial role in conjuring a vivid and rich fantastical world. Employ descriptive details to create vivid mental images and help readers envision the universe you're describing. Here are some tips:

Engage all five senses: instead of focusing solely on sight, appeal to all five senses. Describe the smells, sounds, textures, and even tastes to immerse the reader in the atmosphere.

Avoid descriptive overload: too many descriptions can become overwhelming. Choose details carefully, selecting those that are most significant to the story and ambiance.

Create evocative imagery: use metaphors and comparisons to craft evocative images that transport readers into the fantasy world.

2. Creating evocative language

The choice of words and language plays a major role in establishing a magical atmosphere. Here are some strategies for using evocative language:

Names and terminology: invent names, terms, and expressions specific to your fantastical world to enhance immersion.

Distinctive dialogue: tailor the language and dialogue style of characters to their culture, era, or race, creating authentic and memorable conversations.

Poetic imagery: use poetic writing to describe magical elements, enchanting landscapes, or transcendent moments.

Symbolism and metaphor: integrate symbolic and metaphorical elements into the text to reinforce the story's themes.

3. Building an emotional atmosphere

Fantasy is often associated with strong emotions, whether it be wonder, fear, hope, or melancholy. Use writing style to evoke these emotions in readers:

Character introspection: dive into the thoughts and emotions of characters to allow readers to feel what they are experiencing.

Create moving moments: use emotional descriptions to craft moving moments that touch the reader's heart.

Magical atmosphere: utilize writing style to create a magical atmosphere, describing how magic infiltrates the world and affects the characters.

Craft memorable events: use language to make events memorable and impactful, enhancing the significance of key scenes.

4. The rhythm and cadence

The rhythm and cadence of writing are important for creating a magical atmosphere. Alternate between slow and contemplative passages and moments of fast-paced action to maintain readers' interest. Use short sentences to build tension and longer sentences to evoke reflection.

Writing style is a powerful tool for creating a magical and immersive atmosphere in your fantasy narrative. By using descriptions along with evocative language and building an emotional atmosphere, you can transport your readers into a fantastical world rich in details and emotions.

Chapter 13

Using language to bring your world to life

Creating a language specific to your fantasy world can add a unique depth and authenticity to your narrative. We will explore how to use language to breathe life into your fantastical world and its cultures.

1. Creating an imaginary language

Creating an imaginary language is a complex yet rewarding process. Here are some steps to guide you:

Invent words: start by inventing words for objects, places, creatures, and concepts specific to your fantastical world.

Grammar and syntax: develop a grammar and syntax unique to your language, creating rules for sentence formation, verb tenses, and agreements.

Sound and pronunciation: determine how words in your imaginary language are pronounced, creating distinct systems of sounds and intonations.

Writing and alphabet: if your fantastical world has a unique writing system, create an alphabet or writing unique to it.

Idiomatic expressions: develop idiomatic expressions and proverbs specific to your culture or fictional race.

2. Integration into the narrative

Once you've created your imaginary language, skillfully integrate it into the narrative:

Dialogues: use the imaginary language in character dialogues, ensuring it sounds natural and fluid.

Selective translation: don't force readers to translate everything. Integrate translated or explanatory elements occasionally to facilitate understanding.

Contextual use: use the imaginary language in a way that is relevant to the scene or context. For example, during magical rituals, important conversations, or in specific locations.

Character personalities: characters in your fantastical world may speak the language differently based on their education, race, or social status.

Language evolution: if your fantastical world has a long history, evolve the language over time to reflect cultural and social changes.

3. Creation of dialects and secondary languages

In addition to the main language, you can create dialects or secondary languages specific to certain regions or cultural groups in your fantastical world. This enriches the linguistic diversity of your universe.

4. Symbols and mystery

The imaginary language can also be used to create symbols and mysteries. Characters may discover ancient inscriptions, coded scrolls, or enigmatic poems in the language of their world, adding an additional dimension to the plot.

Creating an imaginary language for your fantastical world is a powerful way to breathe life into your universe and ground it in its own reality. It can enhance reader immersion and add cultural depth to your narrative. However, the use of the imaginary language must be balanced to avoid becoming an obstacle to understanding.

Chapter 14

The author's voice

The author's voice is a fundamental element of any narrative, including in fantasy. It encompasses the style, perspective, and tone that define how the story is told. We will explore how to find and develop your own authorial voice while writing fantasy.

1. Finding your authorial voice

The author's voice is the unique way in which a writer tells a story. Here's how to find yours when writing fantasy:

Reading and inspiration: read extensively in the fantasy genre for inspiration, but do not copy. Identify what attracts you to these narratives and how you could adapt them to your own style.

Express your personality: your authorial voice should reflect your personality and values. Be authentic and true to yourself.

Writing style: develop a writing style that is distinctly yours. It can be descriptive, poetic, fast-paced, humorous, or any style that suits you.

Tone: define the tone of your narrative. Fantasy can be serious, light-hearted, dark, humorous, or a combination of these elements. Choose the tone that best serves your story.

Point of view: choose a narrative point of view that aligns with your authorial voice. First person, third person, or even a multiple point of view can be used to create different effects.

2. Creating a coherent atmosphere

The author's voice should contribute to the atmosphere of your fantasy world. Here's how to achieve that:

Consistency in style: ensure that your writing style remains consistent throughout the story. Readers should be immersed in your universe from the first pages.

Adhere to the tone: the tone you choose should be maintained throughout the narrative. For example, if you opt for a dark atmosphere, don't suddenly introduce light-hearted humor without reason.

Genre conformity: your authorial voice should be suitable for the fantasy genre. It can be epic, mysterious, wondrous, or emotional, depending on the atmosphere you want to create.

Voice evolution: allow your voice to evolve with the plot and characters. If the characters change throughout the story, your voice can evolve to reflect these changes.

3. Personalization and originality

Your authorial voice should be personal and original. Avoid falling into common clichés or stereotypes of the genre. Create a voice that sets you apart from other fantasy writers.

4. Consistency and coherence

Consistency and coherence in your authorial voice are essential to maintain reader immersion. Review and revise your work to ensure that your voice remains constant throughout the story.

Your authorial voice is a distinctive element that brings your fantasy narrative to life. By finding your own voice, creating a consistent atmosphere, personalizing your style, and staying true to your vision, you can captivate readers and transport them into unforgettable fantastical worlds.

Part 6

Monsters, creatures, and races

Chapter 15

Creation of mythical creatures and monsters

Mythical creatures and monsters are iconic elements of fantasy. We will explore how to create original and memorable creatures to enrich your fantasy world.

1. The importance of creatures in fantasy

Mythical creatures play a crucial role in building your fantasy world. They bring a unique dimension to your narrative by expanding the possibilities of the universe, creating challenges for the characters, and reinforcing the themes of the story.

2. Classic creatures and original creations

Fantasy is rich with classic creatures such as dragons, unicorns, elves, and dwarves. You can choose to use these traditional creatures, but it's important to customize them to make them unique to your world.

If you decide to create original creatures, here are some tips:

Cultural context: creatures can be inspired by the culture of your fantasy world. For example, an aquatic civilization might have unique marine creatures.

Story themes: consider how the creatures fit into the themes of your narrative. They can embody important metaphors or symbols.

Ecology and behavior: create creatures with realistic behaviors and life cycles. How do they hunt, reproduce, and interact with their environment?

Relationships with characters: creatures can be allies, enemies, or protectors of characters. Develop complex and nuanced relationships.

3. Magic and creatures

In fantasy, magic is often closely tied to creatures. Some creatures may be magical by nature, while others may be influenced by the magic of their environment.

Magical creatures: these creatures have innate magical abilities. They can cast spells, shapeshift, or manipulate magic in some way.

Magically altered creatures: magic may have genetically modified or transformed certain creatures, making them more powerful, dangerous, or wondrous.

Magic-influenced creatures by environment: creatures can be influenced by magical places. For example, an enchanted forest may be home to mystical creatures.

4. Consequences and stakes

Mythical creatures and monsters must play a significant role in the story. They can be a source of conflicts, puzzles to solve, or quests to fulfill. Ensure that their inclusion has an impact on the characters and the plot.

The creation of mythical creatures and monsters is a key element of fantasy. Whether choosing to use classic creatures or crafting original ones, integrating magical elements, and ensuring they have consequences on the story, you can breathe life into a rich and captivating fantasy world.

Chapter 16

Fantasy races

Fantasy races are a crucial element of fantasy, bringing diversity and depth to your fictional world. We will explore several iconic fantasy races, how to create them, and how to skillfully integrate them into your narrative.

1. Elves

Elves are often described as elegant and immortal beings. Here are some key elements to consider when creating this fantasy race:

Culture and society: develop a complex culture for the elves. Are they peaceful and nature-bound, or are they proud and warrior-like?

Physical characteristics: elves typically have distinctive features such as pointed ears and great beauty. Consider how these characteristics affect how they are perceived by other characters.

History: create a rich history for the elves, including their origin, past accomplishments, and their role in the history of your world.

2. Dwarves

Dwarves are skilled miners and renowned artisans. Here's what to consider when creating dwarves:

Expertise: dwarves are often associated with craftsmanship and mining. Describe their expertise in these fields.

Appearance: dwarves are typically short, sturdy, and bearded. Use these characteristics to develop their visual identity.

Society: explore the dwarven social structure, clans, hierarchies, and traditions.

3. Orcs

Orcs, also referred to as orques or goblins, though the correspondence for the latter is not always exact and can denote slightly different creatures, are often depicted as brutal and warlike beings. Here are some aspects to consider when creating orcs:

Origin: explore the origin of orcs, their history, and their relationship with other races.

Warrior society: orcs are often fierce warriors. Describe their warrior culture, combat tactics, and traditions.

Individuality: remember that each orc is an individual with motivations, emotions, and personal goals.

4. Other fantasy races

Fantasy is full of many other fantastical races, such as centaurs, giants, fairies, and many more. When creating these races, consider the following:

Unique culture: each race should have a unique culture, customs, and traditions.

Interaction with other races: think about how these races interact with each other, whether they coexist peacefully or are in conflict.

Role in the story: ensure that each race has a significant role in the plot. They can be allies, adversaries, or sources of quests.

5. Avoiding stereotypes

When creating fantastical races, avoid overly simplistic stereotypes. Give them depth by exploring their motivations, internal conflicts, and developments throughout the story.

The creation of fantastical races is a crucial aspect of fantasy. By developing rich cultures, captivating histories, and unique characteristics for these races, you can enrich your imaginary world and provide readers with an immersive experience.

Chapter 17

The diversity of fantastical peoples

Fantasy is a rich and varied genre that presents a multitude of fantastical peoples, each with its own culture, history, and characteristics. We will explore the diversity of fantastical peoples and how to integrate them meaningfully into your imaginary world.

1. The importance of diversity

The diversity of fantastical peoples adds richness and depth to your fictional world. It also reflects the real world by demonstrating that cultural diversity is an undeniable reality.

2. Creating unique peoples

When crafting fantastical races, aim to make them unique and memorable. Here are some aspects to consider:

Culture: develop distinct cultures for each people. Their customs, traditions, religion, and value system should reflect their cultural identity.

History: each people should have its own past, heroes, historical conflicts, and accomplishments. These elements contribute to the depth of the story.

Language: create specific languages for each people or, at the very least, distinct dialects. Language is an essential element of cultural identity.

Appearance: physical characteristics such as size, shape, skin color, and distinctive features contribute to visual diversity.

Relations with other peoples: explore how these peoples interact with each other. They can be allies, enemies, or coexist in peace.

3. Cultural conflicts

Cultural conflicts can be a significant source of tension and intrigue in your fantasy narrative. Cultural differences can lead to misunderstandings, diplomatic conflicts, or wars.

4. Tolerance and inclusion

Fantasy provides an opportunity to explore themes of tolerance and inclusion. Showcase how fantastical peoples, despite their differences, can work together to achieve a common goal.

5. Avoiding clichés

When creating diversity among fantastical peoples, steer clear of stereotypical clichés. Cultures and peoples should not be reduced to simplistic archetypes.

The diversity of fantastical peoples is an essential component of fantasy, breathing life into a rich and complex world. By crafting authentic cultures, compelling stories, and nuanced intercultural relationships, you can enrich your narrative and provide readers with an immersive experience.

Part 7

Magical objects, technology, and artifacts

Chapter 18

The integration of technology

While fantasy is often associated with medieval or ancient worlds, the integration of technology can bring a touch of originality to your imaginary universe. We will explore how to creatively incorporate technology into a fantasy world.

1. Creating a balance

One key to integrating technology into a fantasy world is to maintain a balance between technological elements and magical or traditional elements. Here's how to achieve this:

Historical context: determine the history of technology in your fantasy world. How did it develop, who invented it, and what are its implications?

Aesthetic consistency: ensure that technology aesthetically integrates into the universe. It should have an appearance that aligns with the era and style of your world.

Impact on magic: reflect on the interactions between technology and magic. How can magic influence technology, and vice versa?

Social impact: explore how technology affects the society of your fantasy world. It may create divisions, conflicts, or inequalities.

2. Types of technology

Technology can take various forms in a fantasy world. Here are some examples:

Steam-powered machines: devices powered by steam, from locomotives to industrial machinery.

Advanced craftsmanship: weapons, armor, or magical items created using advanced techniques.

Firearms: primitive or sophisticated firearms, depending on the level of technology.

Communication: advanced communication methods, such as telegraphs or magical messaging systems.

Transportation: mechanical vehicles or enhanced mounts.

3. Conflicts between tradition and technology

Conflicts between tradition and technology can be a source of narrative tension. Characters may be divided between those who embrace technology and those who see it as a threat to ancient traditions.

4. Impact on the plot

Technology can play a key role in the plot of your story. It can be used to solve problems, create obstacles, or reinforce the themes of the narrative.

Integrating technology into a fantasy world is an exciting way to create an original and unique universe. By maintaining aesthetic and narrative balance, exploring social implications, and using technology meaningfully in the plot, you can bring to life a fantasy world that combines the best of both worlds.

Chapter 19

Magical artifacts and enchanted objects

Magical artifacts and enchanted objects are iconic elements of fantasy, capable of capturing the imagination of readers. We will explore how to create magical artifacts and enchanted objects that will enrich your imaginary world.

1. The significance of magical artifacts

Magical artifacts are objects with extraordinary powers, often imbued with ancient magic. They play a central role in many fantasy stories, providing opportunities for quests, plots, and characterization.

2. Creating magical artifacts

When crafting magical artifacts, consider the following aspects:

Origin and history: each artifact should have a fascinating history, explaining how it was created, by whom, and for what purpose.

Powers and limitations: determine the powers of the artifact, as well as its limitations. The artifact's powers should have a significant impact on the plot.

Significance: reflect on the significance of the artifact in the context of your story. It may represent a symbol, a relic, or an object of power.

Quest for the artifact: often, characters embark on quests to find a magical artifact. This can be a powerful narrative driving force.

3. Enchanted objects

Enchanted objects may be less powerful than artifacts, but they still possess unique magical qualities. Here's how to create them memorably:

Magical effects: describe the magical effects of the enchanted object. It could be a sword that glows when danger is near, a ring that grants understanding of languages, or a mirror that reveals the truth.

Creation and enchantment: explore how these objects were created and enchanted. Blacksmiths, enchanters, or mages may be involved.

Previous owners: some enchanted objects have had many owners over the centuries. Explore how they have affected the lives of these individuals.

Relationship with characters: enchanted objects may have special relationships with characters. They could be linked to their destiny, powers, or past.

4. Consequences of artifacts and enchanted objects

Magical artifacts and enchanted objects should have consequences in your story. Their powers can create challenges, moral dilemmas, or crucial choices for the characters.

Magical artifacts and enchanted objects are iconic elements of fantasy, offering endless opportunities for plot and characterization. By creating artifacts and enchanted objects rich in history, meaning, and magical powers, you can bring to life an unforgettable fantasy world.

Part 8

Writing key scenes

Chapter 20

The fight scenes

Combat scenes are an essential element of many fantasy narratives, whether they are epic and magical or realistic and brutal. We'll explore how to write combat scenes that captivate readers and seamlessly fit into your fantasy world.

1. The balance between epic and realistic

Combat in fantasy can range from spectacular and magical to brutal and grounded. Finding the right balance between these two extremes is crucial for creating compelling combat scenes.

Epic battles: epic battles are characterized by magical powers, legendary weapons, and heroic feats. They can be thrilling, but it's essential to maintain consistency and avoid exaggeration.

Realistic combat: realistic combat focuses on tactics, fatigue, and physical consequences. It is often darker and more brutal. Describing the scene with precision is paramount.

2. Preparation and planning

Before writing a combat scene, plan it carefully. Here are some steps to follow:

Know the characters: understand the skills, strengths, and weaknesses of your characters. This will determine how they fight.

Define the objective: identify the purpose of the combat. Are the characters fighting to save someone, protect an artifact, or conquer territory?

Visualize the combat: envision the combat scene in your mind. Where does it take place? What are the positions of the fighters?

Determine the outcome: do you know how the combat concludes? This can help guide the scene.

3. Describing combat

When writing combat scenes, description is crucial. Here are some tips for creating dynamic scenes:

Use the senses: describe what characters see, hear, smell, and feel. This will make the scene more immersive.

Avoid confusion: fights can become chaotic. Ensure the reader can follow the action by describing movements clearly.

Be concise: avoid overly long descriptions of each blow and parry. Be concise but evocative.

Emotion and psychology: don't forget to explore the characters' emotions during the fight. Fear, determination, or doubt can add depth.

Variation in pace: alternate between moments of high intensity and quieter moments to maintain the reader's interest.

4. Consequences of combat

Every combat scene should have consequences for the plot, the characters, or the world. Injuries, losses, or changes in fate should be taken into account.

Combat scenes in fantasy can be moments of intense emotion and thrilling action. By balancing the epic and the realistic, planning carefully, using description effectively, and incorporating meaningful consequences, you can create memorable and captivating fights.

Chapter 21

Emotional moments

Moments of emotion are essential pillars of fantasy, as they allow readers to connect with characters and immerse themselves in the story. We will explore how to create authentic emotional moments, highlighting themes such as love, loss, and sacrifice.

1. The importance of emotional moments

The importance of emotional moments lies in creating emotional connections between readers and characters. They can add depth to the story, strengthen character arcs, and explore universal themes.

2. Love in fantasy

Love can take many forms in fantasy, from romantic love to familial or friendly love. Here's how to represent it authentically:

Relationship development: show how relationships evolve throughout the story. Characters can transition from hostility to friendship, or from friendship to love.

Obstacles to love: obstacles, whether magical, social, or personal, can add tension to a romantic relationship.

Love and growth: love can be a catalyst for character growth. It can inspire them to become better, take risks, or change their destiny.

3. Loss and grief

Moments of loss and grief are powerful emotions in fantasy. Here's how to approach them:

Consequences of grief: explore the consequences of grief on characters. How does it affect them emotionally, mentally, and physically?

Recovery and growth: grief can also be a starting point for characters' recovery and growth. They may find the strength to carry on despite the loss.

Ghosts of the past: past losses can haunt characters and influence their actions in the present.

4. Sacrifice

Sacrifice is a common theme in fantasy, whether it's an act of heroic courage or a difficult choice. Here's how to approach it meaningfully:

Meaning of sacrifice: ensure that the sacrifice has significance in the plot. It should have an impact on the story or other characters.

Difficult choices: show the moral dilemmas that lead to the sacrifice. Characters may face impossible choices.

Consequences: explore the consequences of the sacrifice on the surviving characters. This can create complex character arcs.

5. Key moments of emotion

Emotional moments should be well distributed throughout your story, avoiding overuse. Each moment should be earned and contribute to the plot.

Emotional moments in fantasy are a crucial aspect of creating compelling narratives. By authentically exploring love, loss, and sacrifice, you can enrich your fantastical universe and forge strong emotional connections with readers.

Chapter 22

Dialogue scenes

Dialogue scenes are crucial moments in your fantasy narrative. They allow characters to express themselves, confront each other, reveal secrets, and create mystery. Let's explore how to write dynamic and engaging dialogue scenes, focusing on elements of conflict, revelation, and mystery.

1. The importance of dialogue scenes

Dialogue scenes serve to develop characters, advance the plot, and explore the themes of your story. They provide an opportunity for characters to express themselves and reveal their true nature.

2. Conflict in dialogue scenes

Conflict is a crucial element in fantasy dialogue scenes. Here's how to introduce it effectively:

Objectives and motivations: each character in the scene should have clear goals and motivations. Conflict can arise from the pursuit of these objectives.

Tense dialogues: create tense and engaging dialogues using sharp retorts, fundamental disagreements, and high stakes.

Character development: conflict scenes can be an opportunity to reveal hidden aspects of characters, such as their weaknesses, wounds, or secrets.

3. Revelations

Dialogue scenes are often the ideal place to unveil crucial information. Here's how to handle them:

Dosing revelations: revelations should be carefully dosed. Avoid revealing everything at once and maintain a certain level of mystery.

High stakes: revelations should have significant stakes for the plot or characters.

Character reactions: explore how characters react to the revelations. This can include surprise, anger, betrayal, or understanding.

4. Introducing mystery

Mystery is an intriguing element in fantasy. Here's how to introduce it into dialogue scenes:

Subtle clues: use subtle clues to create mystery. Characters can let slip information without revealing everything.

Unspoken words: the unspoken, silences, and innuendos can enhance mystery. Readers should wonder about what is not said.

Unanswered questions: dialogue scenes can raise unanswered questions, encouraging readers to continue reading for explanations.

5. Conclusions of dialogue scenes

Each dialogue scene should have a meaningful conclusion. This could be an agreement, a disagreement, a decision, or a change in the characters' attitudes.

Dialogue scenes in fantasy are a powerful way to develop characters, advance the plot, and engage readers. By introducing elements of conflict, revelations, and mystery in a balanced way, you can bring dynamic and captivating dialogues to life.

Part 9

Revision and refinement

Chapter 23

Reviewing and editing your manuscript

Revision and editing are essential steps in the writing process, allowing you to refine and perfect your fantasy manuscript. We will explore the key stages of revision and editing, providing you with the tools needed to enhance the quality of your work.

1. The importance of revision and editing

Revision and editing are crucial to ensure that your manuscript reaches its full potential. These stages help you eliminate errors, strengthen consistency, refine style, and enhance the clarity of your narrative.

2. Revision stages

Revision involves reviewing your manuscript as a whole and making structural improvements. Here are some key steps to follow:

Critical reading: start with a critical reading of your manuscript. Identify major issues such as plot inconsistencies or gaps in characterization.

Narrative structure: ensure that the story has a strong narrative structure, including an introduction, development, tension peaks, and a satisfying conclusion.

Characters and development: review the characterization of your characters. Are they consistent? Do they have satisfying character arcs?

Trimming unnecessary scenes: identify scenes that do not contribute to the plot or characterization and consider eliminating them.

Dialogue: review dialogue scenes to ensure they are authentic and meaningful.

3. Editing stages

Editing focuses on correcting details, from grammar to punctuation. Here are some steps for editing:

Grammar and spelling: eliminate grammatical and spelling errors. Use spell-check tools, but don't forget to manually proofread.

Style and clarity: improve writing style by avoiding complex sentences and prioritizing clarity. Ensure that descriptions are vivid, and language is appropriate for the genre.

Dialogue revision: review dialogues to ensure they sound natural and serve the plot or characterization.

Formatting: ensure that the manuscript is correctly formatted with consistent layout.

Continuity: check for plot, character, and fantastical world element continuity.

4. Seeking feedback

It is generally recommended to have others, such as beta readers or editors, read your manuscript to obtain objective feedback. Their perspectives can help you identify issues you may not have noticed.

5. Final step: proofreading

Once you have completed the revision and editing, proofread your manuscript one last time to ensure it is ready for publication. Take your time to identify any final potential errors.

Revision and editing are crucial steps in perfecting your fantasy manuscript. By following these steps, seeking external feedback, and proofreading your work, you can ensure that your narrative is ready to be shared with the world.

Chapter 24

Obtaining feedback and using it

Once you have revised and edited your fantasy manuscript, it is essential to obtain feedback from third parties to further refine your work. We will explore the importance of obtaining feedback and how to use it to enhance your narrative.

1. The importance of external feedback

External feedback is valuable for several reasons:

Objective perspective: external readers bring an objective perspective to your work, which you, as an author, may struggle to have.

Error detection: external feedback can identify errors, inconsistencies, or inaccuracies that you may have missed.

Public reactions: external feedback allows you to understand how your work is perceived by the target audience.

Improvement suggestions: external readers can provide constructive suggestions to enhance your narrative.

2. How to obtain feedback

Here are some sources to obtain feedback:

Beta readers: beta readers are individuals who read your manuscript and provide feedback. They can be friends, members of writing groups, or publishing professionals.

Writing groups: joining a local or online writing group gives you access to a network of peers willing to exchange feedback.

Professional editors: if your budget allows, you can hire a professional editor to review and provide feedback on your work.

Beta readers from your target audience: ask individuals from your target audience to read your manuscript and share their impressions.

3. Asking the right questions

When seeking feedback, be sure to ask specific questions to guide readers in their responses. Here are some examples of useful questions:

- are the characters compelling and well-developed?

- is the plot consistent and well-structured?

- are there parts of the narrative that seem to lag or slow down the action?

- do the dialogues sound natural, and do they contribute to characterization and plot?

- are there inconsistencies or errors in the story?

- are the fantastical elements of the world easily understandable for the reader?

4. Using feedback

Once you've received feedback, it's essential to use it to improve your narrative. Here's how to proceed:

Analyse the feedback: objectively review the feedback. Identify trends or common points.

Prioritize changes: you don't need to follow all feedback to the letter. Prioritize changes based on their relevance and impact on your narrative.

Revise and edit: make the necessary modifications to your manuscript based on the feedback.

Reread: after making changes, reread your work to ensure the modifications integrate well into the overall narrative.

External feedback is a crucial tool for enhancing your fantasy narrative. By seeking feedback from various sources, asking specific questions, and using feedback effectively, you can refine your work and make it even more captivating for your readers.

Chapter 25

Preparing for publication: self-publishing or seeking a publisher

When your fantasy manuscript is ready to be shared with the world, it's time to make crucial decisions regarding publication. We will explore the two main options available to you: self-publishing and seeking a traditional publisher.

1. Self-publishing

Self-publishing is a process in which you independently publish your book without going through a traditional publishing house. Here are some advantages of self-publishing:

Total control: you have complete control over the content, cover, and promotion of your book.

Speed: you can publish your book more quickly than through a traditional publishing house.

Greater share of profits: you retain a larger share of the profits from the sale of your book.

Accessibility: self-publishing provides an opportunity for unpublished or independent authors to enter the market.

However, self-publishing also comes with challenges, including the need to handle all aspects of publishing, promoting, and distributing your book on your own.

2. Seeking a traditional publisher

If you choose to seek a traditional publisher, here are some advantages to consider:

Validation: being published by a traditional publishing house can be seen as validation of your work.

Extended distribution: publishers have established distribution networks that can help your book reach a wider audience.

Professional support: you benefit from the expertise of professional editors, proofreaders, and cover designers.

However, seeking a traditional publisher can be a lengthy and competitive process, and you will need to share a portion of the profits with the publisher.

3. Personal decision

The decision between self-publishing and seeking a traditional publisher depends on your personal goals, resources, and preferences. Here are some questions to consider:

- what are your publishing goals?

- are you willing to take on the responsibility of publishing and promoting your book?

- do you have the financial resources for self-publishing, or do you prefer the financial support of a publisher?

- are you prepared to dedicate time to seeking a traditional publisher and negotiating contracts?

4. The publication process

Regardless of the path you choose, here are some key steps to prepare your book for publication. If you opt for a traditional publisher, some of these steps may be handled by them:

Final proofreading and editing: ensure your manuscript is free of errors.

Cover design: create or have designed an appealing cover for your book.

Formatting: format your book for print or digital publication.

Promotion: develop a promotion plan to reach your target audience.

Distribution: determine how you will distribute your book, whether online or in print.

Preparing for publication is an exciting step in the journey of any fantasy author. Whether you choose self-publishing or seek a traditional publisher, it's important to weigh the pros and cons of each option to choose the one that best aligns with your goals and creative vision.

Part 10

Promote and share

Chapter 26

Marketing strategies

Once you have published your fantasy book, it is essential to implement marketing strategies to attract readers' attention. We will explore various marketing strategies for fantasy authors.

1. Building an author platform

Before implementing marketing strategies, it's important to establish a strong author platform. This includes:

Author website: create a professional website to promote your work, share information about yourself and your books, and engage with readers.

Social media: use social media to build an online presence. Share relevant content, interact with your readers, and promote your work.

Newsletter: collect email addresses and create a newsletter to keep your readers informed about new releases, events, and special offers.

2. Book promotion

Here are some specific marketing strategies to promote your fantasy book:

Reviews and blogs: send free copies of your book to bloggers and literary reviewers specializing in fantasy to obtain reviews.

Contests and free giveaways: organize online contests or free giveaways to attract new readers.

Cross-promotion: collaborate with other fantasy authors to mutually promote your works.

Participation in book fairs: make sure to participate in book fairs, conferences, or fantasy conventions to meet readers in person.

Online advertising: use online advertising on social media or platforms like amazon to reach a broader audience.

3. Additional content

Create additional content to engage readers and encourage them to learn more about your fantasy universe:

Short stories: write short stories or bonus stories related to your fantasy world.

Blog: maintain a blog on topics related to fantasy, such as writing, world-building, or book analyses.

Visual art: share illustrations, maps, or other visual elements of your fantasy world.

4. Engaging with your audience

Regularly interact with your readers by responding to their comments, participating in social media discussions, and being accessible and authentic. An engaged community can become one of your greatest assets.

5. Measuring effectiveness

Make sure to track the effectiveness of your marketing strategies. Use analytics tools to monitor audience growth, sales numbers, and social media engagement. Adjust your strategies based on the results you achieve.

Promoting your fantasy book is a crucial step in reaching a wider audience. By combining the creation of a strong author platform, targeted promotional strategies, and engagement with your readers, you can maximize the impact of your work.

Chapter 27

Connecting with the fantasy community

The fantasy community is a dynamic and passionate network of authors, readers, and enthusiasts of the genre. Connecting with this community can be extremely beneficial for fantasy authors. We will explore ways for you to get involved and build strong relationships within the fantasy community.

1. The benefits of connection

The benefits of connecting with the fantasy community are numerous, including:

Support and encouragement: the fantasy community provides valuable support to authors in the form of advice, encouragement, and constructive feedback.

Networking: you can establish professional relationships with other authors, editors, and industry professionals.

Inspiration: the community can inspire you, provide new ideas, and keep you informed about the latest trends in the genre.

Promotion: you can promote your work within the community and reach an audience already passionate about fantasy.

2. How to connect

Here are some ways to connect with the fantasy community:

Online groups: join discussion groups, forums, or social media dedicated to fantasy. Engage in conversations, share your experience, and ask questions.

Events and conventions: attend fantasy events, conferences, and conventions. It's the perfect opportunity to meet other enthusiasts of the genre.

Collaborative writing: collaborate with other fantasy authors on collaborative writing projects. This can strengthen your skills and expand your network.

Reviews and beta reading: offer to read and critique the works of other fantasy authors. In return, seek reviews for your own work.

Blogging and podcasting: if you enjoy writing or talking about fantasy, start a blog or podcast dedicated to the genre. This will help you attract a passionate audience.

Local writing groups: look for local writing groups or writing workshops dedicated to fantasy. You can meet other authors in your area.

3. Sharing and contribution

When connecting with the fantasy community, it's important not only to seek to receive but also to give. Share your knowledge, expertise, and passion with others. Actively contributing to the community strengthens the bonds you create.

4. Respect and ethics

Always respect the opinions and experiences of other members of the community. Be respectful in your critiques and comments. Ethics are essential to maintain good relationships within the community.

The fantasy community is a rich place in resources and opportunities for authors passionate about the genre. By connecting with other authors and readers, you can enrich your writing experience, benefit from valuable support, and expand your professional network.

Chapter 28

Recap of key points

From creating your fantastical world to publishing your work, you've learned, throughout these pages, about the elements that make fantasy a unique and captivating genre. Now, as we conclude this guide, let's reflect on the key points that have marked your journey as a fantasy author.

1. The importance of creativity

Fantasy is a genre that relies on creativity and imagination. You've learned how to create a fantastical world rich in details, history, culture, and magic. Your ability to invent unique worlds and bring memorable characters to life is at the core of fantasy writing.

2. Understanding archetypes

You have explored the classical archetypes that populate the world of fantasy, such as heroes, anti-heroes, antagonists, mythical creatures, and fantastical races. Understanding these archetypes allows you to play with reader expectations while building compelling characters.

3. Narrative structure

Narrative structure is a key element of any fantastical tale. You have learned to design strong plots, create epic quests, and incorporate elements of history into your narrative. A well-constructed structure keeps the reader's attention and immerses them in your fantastical world.

4. Character psychology

The psychology of fantastical characters is a fascinating field. You have explored the motivations, inner conflicts, and character arcs that make characters credible and human, even in a fantastical world.

5. Writing style

Writing style in fantasy is crucial to create a magical atmosphere. You have learned to use language evocatively, create visual descriptions, and establish a distinctive authorial voice for your work.

6. Connecting with the community

Connecting with the fantasy community is a key step for any author. You have discovered the benefits of support, inspiration, and networking within this passionate community.

7. Publication and marketing

You have explored publishing options, whether through self-publishing or seeking a traditional publisher. You have also learned how to implement marketing strategies to promote your fantasy book.

8. The rest is up to you

You now have the knowledge to write a great fantasy book. Keep writing, creating, connecting with other enthusiasts, and nurturing your love for this extraordinary genre. You have the ability to create magical worlds, captivate readers, and bring unforgettable characters to life. Don't hesitate, dive in.

Table of contents

Foreword..7
Part 1 – Introduction to fantasy................................11
  Chapter 1 – The essential elements of fantasy........13
  Chapter 2 – The evolution of fantasy and its subgenres..16
Part 2 – Planning and preparation...............................20
  Chapter 3 – Finding inspiration for your fantasy world..22
  Chapter 4 – Creating your world: geography, history, and culture...25
  Chapter 5 – Creating a magic system.....................29
Part 3 – Memorable characters...................................32
  Chapter 6 – Creating fantasy characters.................34
  Chapter 7 – The evolution of your characters........38
  Chapter 8 – The psychology of characters.............42
Part 4 – Narrative structure...46
  Chapter 9 – The basic structure..............................48
  Chapter 10 – Quests and the chosen one's journey.51
  Chapter 11 – Secondary plots and subtexts............54
Part 5 – Writing and style..59
  Chapter 12 – The writing style in fantasy...............61
  Chapter 13 – Using language to bring your world to life..64
  Chapter 14 – The author's voice.............................67
Part 6 – Monsters, creatures, and races.......................70
  Chapter 15 – Creation of mythical creatures and monsters...72
  Chapter 16 – Fantasy races.....................................75
  Chapter 17 – The diversity of fantastical peoples. .78
Part 7 – Magical objects, technology, and artifacts.....81
  Chapter 18 – The integration of technology...........83

Chapter 19 – Magical artifacts and enchanted objects..86
Part 8 – Writing key scenes..89
Chapter 20 – The fight scenes...............................91
Chapter 21 – Emotional moments.........................94
Chapter 22 – Dialogue scenes................................97
Part 9 – Revision and refinement.............................101
Chapter 23 – Reviewing and editing your manuscript..103
Chapter 24 – Obtaining feedback and using it......106
Chapter 25 – Preparing for publication: self-publishing or seeking a publisher........................110
Part 10 – Promote and share.....................................115
Chapter 26 – Marketing strategies........................117
Chapter 27 – Connecting with the fantasy community...120
Chapter 28 – Recap of key points........................123

Contents

FOREWORD	VII
One	3
Two	9
Three	17
Four	25
Five	31
Six	37
Seven	45
Eight	49
Nine	55
Ten	59
Eleven	67
Twelve	73
Thirteen	79
Fourteen	83
Fifteen	97
Sixteen	103
Seventeen	109
Eighteen	115

Nineteen	119
Twenty	123
MARGINALIA	125
APPENDICES	127
SELECT BIBLIOGRAPHY	135

Foreword

I published a book in the summer of 2019 which had for a title the *Hidden Faces* behind the attack on New York, on 9/11. The title was Salvador Dali's own given by him to his one novel written in north-east America in the 1940s. My book, it was on the short side – I intended at the time to write a follow-up volume, this is it – had mostly dealt with the planes in New York in 2001, the parties involved in the attack. Nothing to do with the Covid pandemic, for it had not yet begun. I was somewhat taken aback – since I reasoned even if I was right that the attack on New York was hidden in plain narrative, it was now in the past - to have very negative feedback. On the back cover of *Hidden Faces* I wrote that the attack on New York was coded using two well-known texts: Shakespeare's last play *The Tempest* and Lewis Carroll's *Alice in Wonderland*. As said, I had no concern at the time that there would be threats issued – even if I was right and the New York planes were hidden not so much in plain sight but narrative – but later, on reading the name of the first man to be injected with Pfizer in Coventry, that he was a William Shakespeare, I began to take a much harder look at both 9/11 and the Covid pandemic, to treat them as one event, two acts of evil in the performance of the same play. So this second

THE PLAGUE DOCTOR

---

book is an update to *Hidden Faces*, it includes a decoding of related texts only begun in 2019, and the proof of what was still a strong suspicion only, five years ago.

M. BOUTFLOWER, April, 2025

The Plague Doctor

One

Ask Lewis Carroll where he got the orange marmalade from in *Alice in Wonderland* and he could end up in prison for making a false statement. Later in this book, I will suggest that you ask someone in the government where they got a 'conspiracy theory' from, but first things first. If I tell you the letter 'c' in Shakespeare's play is to be seen or unseen, to be deleted or reinstated, how would that help the reader in discovering the mad hatter in Wonderland in the play? What word would you search for first? I would suggest it would be the verb, to chatter... Cheshire Cat? Hatter first. Enter Caliban in scene two of Act Two of the play.

2.2 Enter CALIBAN, with a burden of wood; a noise of thunder heard.

CALIBAN
All the infections that the sun sucks up
From bogs, fens, flats, on Prosper fall and make him
By inchmeal a disease! His spirits hear me
And yet I needs must curse. But they'll nor pinch,

THE PLAGUE DOCTOR

Fright me with urchin—shows, pitch me i' the mire,
Nor lead me, like a firebrand, in the dark
Out of my way, unless he bid 'em; but
For every trifle are they set upon me;
Sometime like apes that mow and chatter at me
And after bite me, then like hedgehogs which
Lie tumbling in my barefoot way and mount
Their pricks at my footfall; sometime am I
All wound with adders who with cloven tongues
Do hiss me into madness

This book is being written in real time by you the reader. How many of you think you know what 'to mow' means? A show of mouses on their pads, not hands...

BAREFOOT, PAW?

Not what I was looking for...

BY INCHMEAL A DISEASE, MALADE, MARMALADE...

Mouse or rat is it? Inch-malade-isease. In chapter seven of *Alice's Adventures in Wonderland* she wonders if the dormouse is right about the three sisters, Liddell ones, in the treacle well, that they lived on a diet of treacle. The sleepy dormouse starts abruptly with its tale.

'Once upon a time there were three little sisters,' the Dormouse

❧ THE PLAGUE DOCTOR ☙

began in a great hurry, 'and their names were Elsie, Lacie, and Tillie, and they lived at the bottom of a well –'

'What did they live on?' said Alice, who always took a great interest in questions of eating and drinking.

'They lived on treacle,' said the Dormouse, after thinking for a minute or two.

'They couldn't have done that, you know,' Alice gently remarked; 'they'd have been ill.'

'So they were,' said the Dormouse, 'very ill.'

Tres malade... marmalade. Who is Marma Leda? The mother of Humpty Dumpty. It should be said in passing that the treacle ideally is to be taken intravenously, by needle; but don't worry, we already know that Alice has a thimble to ward any needle off. If you are starting to wonder if there is foul play afoot, you'd be right, Lewis Carroll a distant cousin of mine is eminently blackmailable, plus he has his third eye open and can therefore see outside of linear time into the future, our present... Disease? In the play within the play, the deities are given their Roman names. There is a reason for this that we will get to soon enough. In the interlude, Ceres, Greek Demeter, asks Iris if Venus will be at the wedding of Miranda to Ferdinand?

CERES   *Tell me, heavenly bow,*
   If Venus or her son, as thou dost know,
   Do now attend the queen? Since they did plot
   The means that dusky Dis my daughter got,

❧ THE PLAGUE DOCTOR ☙

Her and her blind boy's scandaled company
I have forsworn.

Dis is the Roman name for the god of the underworld, Greek Hades, 'dis' being the contraction of *dius*, *divus* or *deus*, all of which mean 'divine'. Dis is dark Pluto, the richest of all the gods. In myth – if not in reality – Pluto aided and abetted by Venus and Cupid, kidnaps Ceres' daughter Proserpina, keeping her in the underworld for half of every year, the barren half above ground. Why does this aside matter? Because Proserpina is code for the real author of the play, and, when she returns, the earth bears fruit. She is therefore the productive one. Alice's adventures were originally to have been 'underground'. Proserpina, Prospero? You're on the right track, headed in the right direction. Abetted? Why did the geoengineer in the film of *The Avengers* [1998] offer to 'double the bet' in his game of croquet with blind 'Father' at Blindheim? Because he had a former career in cloning. He has an armband with what looks a snake on, just where you would take the treacle, your medicine, intravenously... Who is Proserpina really? We'll get to her, one of her at any rate. The Dormouse, a rat? Why do you think that? If you are headed in the wrong direction, you may run into the Queen of Hearts who will have your head off. Is she quite real? Yes, I can vouch for that... While we are at 'A Mad Tea-Party', letter-t party?, why does Alice say this to the Hatter?

'You should learn not to make personal remarks,' Alice said with some severity: 'it's very rude.'

THE PLAGUE DOCTOR

A clue? A location in the Peleponnese, and an anagram or two. A third party? The hatter, the Cheshire Cat, without the C's? In Act One of *The Tempest*, Miranda, daughter of Prospero, who was the duke of Milan until usurped by his brother Antonio, asks her father who she is after all these sonnets and plays? – or words to that effect. In the conversation that follows, Prospero asks if she recalls anything of her early life spent in Milan?

MIRANDA *[to Prospero]*   ... *Had I not*
  Four or five women once that tended me?

4 + 5 + on[c]e = ten-ded

The 'c' in once is to be deleted... How do we know which letter 'c's' in the play are meant to be deleted? Did Shakespeare think of chatter as someone with a hat on? Later in Act One, Prospero is in conversation with his familiar Ariel.

PROSPERO *[to Ariel]*   ... *Then was this island*
  [Save for the son that she did litter here,
  A freckled whelp, hag-born] not honoured with
  A human shape.

ARIEL   *Yes, Caliban, her son.*

THE PLAGUE DOCTOR

PROSPERO
> *Dull thing, I say so – he, that Caliban,*
> *Whom now I keep in service...*

No 'y' in kee... Son, or French *chose*? *so-c-he*... Shape-ARIEL? So there is 'c' that needs reinstating and another that needs deleting. Academics and others not yet with it, comment that Shakespeare has lost the plot, forgot where he was going with it, elsewhere in the play, when there is a child who is not mentioned before, who pops or crops up. The anagram of learn is Lerna, where the Hydra comes from? Identity is difficult to discern in both the play and Wonderland. The Hydra grows back two heads for every one cut off – unless Hercules in his Second Labour has with him his nephew Iolaus to cauterise the stumps – and one head is immortal: Hercules has to bury it deep under a rock. Did he fail in his Second Labour for the reason that he got help or that the Hydra is immortal? If you know Python, the Athenian potter, not Pythia's, then you will have seen that what is depicted on Douris' cup – potted by Python – differs markedly from the later telling of Jason's encounter with a serpent: he is being initiated with Athena looking on, presiding. So, is Hercules, his encounter with the Hydra, more about an internal process within the etheric body, that will enable the semi-divine Hercules to be counted among the gods, the immortals? Now, I see that not much progress has been made in decoding Caiban's speech. We will give the reader a second chance in chapter two, and maybe a third if needed in chapter three.

Two

2.2 Enter CALIBAN, with a burden of wood; a noise of thunder heard.

CALIBAN

All the infections that the sun sucks up
From bogs, fens, flats, on Prosper fall and make him
By inchmeal a disease! His spirits hear me
And yet I needs must curse. But they'll nor pinch,
Fright me with urchin—shows, pitch me i' the mire,
Nor lead me, like a firebrand, in the dark
Out of my way, unless he bid 'em; but
For every trifle are they set upon me;
Sometime like apes that mow and chatter at me
And after bite me, then like hedgehogs which
Lie tumbling in my barefoot way and mount
Their pricks at my footfall; sometime am I
All wound with adders who with cloven tongues
Do hiss me into madness

In the eighteenth and nineteenth centuries engravings would

THE PLAGUE DOCTOR

have Caliban at the mouth of a cave with snakes twisted about his body... A clue? Before Caliban enters, Ariel, the play's airy spirit, ends scene one with talk of King Alonso's son, Ferdinand whom is feared drowned in a tempest that in good time proves illusory, to have been so.

ARIEL

Prospero, my lord, shall know what I have done;
So King, go safely on to seek thy son.

Any thoughts on the matter or ether of Ariel's speech? The son sucks up? Back in Act One, Prospero is telling his daughter Miranda of her 'false uncle' Antonio, the usurping duke of Milan. Having told her, reminded her that he'd been the prime Duke, he then lays into her Uncle Antonio, *Tio Anon*? Fals-une-cle, Fal-sone-*cle*.

PROSPERO

Being once perfected how to grant suits,
How to deny them, who t'advance, and who
To trash for overtopping, new created
The creatures that were mine, I say, or changed 'em,
Or else new formed 'em, having both the key
Of officer and office, set all hearts i'th' state
To what tune pleased his ear, that now he was
The ivy which had hid my princely trunk
And sucked my verdure out on't. Thou attend'st not.

THE PLAGUE DOCTOR

MIRANDA
  O, good sir, I do.

PROSPERO   I pray thee, mark me.

Being one perfected, like a Cathar? Mark me, if Prospero is not the beast, Caliban? This is an inquisition into scaled identity, the play is...

C-INQUISITION, SUITS
WHICH, WITCH, SYCORAX

Sycorax? The play's witch, who litters Caliban on the island deserted island and then dies. KORE or Kora is Greek for a maiden. Proserpina, prior to her being kidnapped, is spoken of, written down as a maiden, the one. Corax?

CORVUS CORAX

Latin for a corvid, raven... If this is an inquisition, with a reinstated 'c', what does that make *the ivy which*...

F-IVY WITCH...

THAT NOW HE WAS THE IVY WHICH HAD HID...

SPANISH *HIEDRA* [HAD HID] PORTUGUESE *HERA*...

THE PLAGUE DOCTOR

In the interlude Hera is Roman Juno. Hera breeds the Hydra to kill Hercules, her husband's natural son with a mortal.

MAINTENANT, HAND TENANT...
MAIN-TEN-FOURMI F-IVY...
FOUR OR FIVE WOMEN ONCE THAT TENDED ME...

Me, Miranda... Confirmation of F-ivy, the Hydra being the solution to the play's inquisition.

WHICH, WITCH, SUI[T]S, INQUISITION...

So Miranda in scene two of Act One says to her father: Would you please tell me who I am? After all, this is the last play and I've got nowhere with who I am, to date... Or words to that effect:

MIRANDA *You have often*
  Begun to tell me what I am, but stopped
  And left me to a bootless inquisition,
  Concluding, 'Stay, not yet.'

THAT TENDED, DE-TEN, OFTEN...
VOUS-AVEZ SOU-VENT...

The Baconians or Baconites, they've long since spotted the acrostic coming down the left-hand side of the above, that it makes:

◆§ THE PLAGUE DOCTOR §◆

FRANCIS BACON-CLUDING

Concluding, Dull thing? Francis – not his brother Anthony who is about to be burnt alive for buggery of French boys; only the intervention of the French king spares him an ignoble death. He is preoccupied with his concern that news of his activities will have reached the Elizabethan court. For a moment, take your eyes off Caliban, his speech, and look at line two of her Miranda's speech above... Someone, anyone? Four hundred years and counting... The dark forces, they are relying on our inability to crack the code embedded in the play. They can say or would like to, 'We told you so,' what they were up to in the most famous of plays – so you couldn't say you hadn't seen it - and you went along with our nefarious schemes in approval of them.

I AM, BUT
I AM, MAIS
JE SUIS, MAIS
JE SU-IS SOU-VENT, FOU HATTER?
JE SU-IS-SANS BOTTES C-INQUISITION...

Mais-stopped, stay not... Prospero ends his speech to come with *thou mayst*, Miranda mayst... Add or subtract letter 'c'?

MIRANDA *You have often*
  Begun to tell me what I am, but stopped
  And c-left me two a bootless c-inquisition,
  Con[c]luding, 'Stay, pas en-c-ore.'

THE PLAGUE DOCTOR

ENCORE
ONCERE
BACON-*LUDENS*
PAS-EN[C]ORE...

C-oncle or suncle? In chapter three we will learn of the interchangeability of letter 'l' and 'r' in the play – this in order to have the daughter, Miranda, morph into the duke of Milan... The golden key on the glass table at the bottom of the rabbit-hole:

ENCORE
ENCOLE
ENOCLE
CLE OR

STOP-PED[PIED]
SANS BOTTES
PAS PAS

STAY, MAYST, REMAIN, GERMAIN?
STAY [PAS] ENCORE
SYCORAT[H]ENE, SYCORAX

Goddess Athene, who shakes her spear, likes to...

PAS-EN[C]ORE, PEARSONE

THE PLAGUE DOCTOR

Miranda is an anagram of Mainard the spelling of which is fluid for the Tudor: an alternative version is Maynard. Who – out of the Lord Chamberlain's players, actors – is someone née Pearson going to choose to hide behind? William Shakespeare, son of Mary Arden, the father of Susannah... Susan/na Maynard, née Pearson, married to Henry Maynard, principal secretary to William Cecil, Lord Treasurer. His mother is given as Dorothy Perrot. Any more thoughts on Caliban his speech? Maugrim... The chief of the Narnian police? How so? Maw, mouth, morgue, grim... you've lost me... Grimace? L to R, no G. We shall get to the letter G, its omission, in good time. A hint? Mow is the first syllable of a first name. No not a Christian one... The ace in Alice's pack of cards? Not yet. Hiss me into medness? Medusa? For every trifle? Four, three? No rifles in Shakespeare's day. Baatelle? Bagatelle?... Barefoot way, paw way. Wound *herida*? Adder, Hydra? Tri-fell? *Herida, herissone...*

AND-AFTER, DAPRES, L to R, UNLESS APES...
CHAPELIER, LIE TUMBLING, LE LIERRE, ALI[C]E, A LIE?
T-HAT BEAUTEOUS... CHAPEAU....

Sonnet X? I'll need to have a read of it.

SEA-KING T-HAT BEAUTEOUS... CHAPEAU.... ROINATE?

Three

It is time for Prospero to inform his daughter, bodily, become her and vice versa...

PROSPERO   'Tis time
   I should inform thee farther. Lend thy hand
   And pluck my magic garment from me. So,
   Lie there, my art.—Wipe thou thine eyes. Have comfort.
   The direful spectacle of the wrack, which touched
   The very virtue of compassion in thee,
   I have with such provision in mine art
   So safely ordered that there is no soul—
   No, not so much perdition as an hair,
   Betid to any creature in the vessel
   Which thou heard'st cry, which thou saw'st sink. Sit down,
   For thou must now know farther.

MIRANDA   You have often
   Begun to tell me what I am, but stopped
   And left me to a bootless inquisition,
   Concluding, 'Stay. Not yet.'

THE PLAGUE DOCTOR

PROSPERO   *The hour's now come;*
The very minute bids thee ope thine ear.
Obey, and be attentive. Canst thou remember
A time before we came unto this cell?
I do not think thou canst, for then thou wast not
Out three years old.

MIRANDA   *Certainly, sir, I can.*

PROSPERO
By what? By any other house or person?
Of anything the image tell me that
Hath kept with thy remembrance.

MIRANDA   *'Tis far off*
And rather like a dream than an assurance
That my remembrance warrants. Had I not
Four or five women once that tended me?

Lie there, my art... To the Oxfordian this is insider knowledge of the kind Edward de Vere as earl of Oxford, would know of his estranged father-in-law William Cecil, Lord Treasurer. How would the likes of the actor, not playwright, William Shakespeare, know that at the end of his working day, William Cecil, would think to say, 'Lie there...' as he steps out of his robe of office, day job? A Thomas Fuller reported that Elizabeth's closest advisor, William Cecil, 'At night when he put off his gown, ... used to say, "Lie there, Lord Treasurer."'

THE PLAGUE DOCTOR

So had Fuller learnt of this routine of Henry's employer from Secretary Maynard? We don't know. Why did Miranda have to be three years old on leaving Milan? We can tell why... Think of a number between one and hundred that when divided into the next three in sequence generates six? Miranda is pretty sure she had four women or five that tended her, that is before she and her father were cast adrift to be washed up on the island Caliban thinks his own, he inherits from Sycorax... yes, which is reason enough for him to curse Prospero... Well then, answer me this. Why in what expert opinion has down as being the last play in the canon, would de Vere leave in an anagram of his father-in-law's secretary?

PROSPERO
Thou hadst, and more, Miranda, but how is it...

1 [ ] 3, 4, 5 and more
  2   12   6

PROSPERO
Twelve year since, Miranda, twelve year since,
Thy father was the Duke of Milan and
A prince of power.

12th letter L
18th letter R

miLand and a ... miRanda...

THE PLAGUE DOCTOR

They have changed eyes as would Ferdinand and Miranda, over a game of chess. Two heads of the one Hydra...

COVID-19, COVID1819, CORVIDS, SYCORAX...

What consituted the curse? Let me find the place...

CALIBAN
> You taught me language, and my profit on't
> Is I know how to curse. The red plague rid you
> For learning me your language.

Not yet, toadavia no, de Vere? *Sapo*, verdure, vere dur... Main-ard. Avian flu? Who were the first two people to be injected with what was a vaccine in name only, Lady first?

MARGARET KEENAN
WILLIAM SHAKESPEARE

Where were they? Coven-tree by Nurse May Parsons, formerly of the Philippines, an innocent abroad.

MARG-ARET-CLE-NAN
MARG-TREA-CLE-NAN

Why have the Dodo [alias Charles Dodgson, Oxford don] adopt the posture that Shakespeare is supposed to have been known for, when he, Dodo, considers who has won the race

THE PLAGUE DOCTOR

just run? The caucus-race in chapter three, yes? The rest waited in silence, s? At last, enfin, Dodo decides.

The question the Dodo could not answer without a great deal of thought, and it sat for a long time with one finger pressed upon its forehead [the position you usually see Shakespeare, in the pictures of him], while the rest waited in silence. At last the Dodo said, 'Everybody has won, and all must have prizes?'

'But who is to give the prizes?' quite a chorus of voices asked.

'Why, she, of course,' said the Dodo, pointing to Alice with one finger, and the whole party at once crowded round her, calling out in a confused way, 'Prizes! Prizes!'

Alice had no idea what to do, and in despair she put her hand in her pocket, and pulled out a box of comfits [luckily the salt water had not got into it], and handed them round as prizes. There was exactly one apiece, all round.

Dodgson alias Lewis Carroll, he'd been lucky to get John Tenniel, the *Punch* illustrator, to work on *Alice Through The Looking-glass*. Having complained of the poor quality of the first print-run *of Alice's Adventures in Wonderland*, he must have become fed up by the details that Carroll saw as being so important. Tenniel told Dodgson at one point that he didn't need advice on models to use as he generated images mentally, drew from a mental realm for inspiration... Apiece? There are two illustrations for chapter three, both with a monkey in, though there is no obvious reason for an ape to appear in the chapter at all. In the first, the monkey's features

THE PLAGUE DOCTOR

are so edited, cropped off that he might have the profile of an eagle. In a second illustration the monkey looks out over the Dodo's hunched back somewhat incongruously. Finger or *singe*? – because it is easy for a mistake to be made discerning if it is an 's' or 'f' in a font, a typeface of the Tudors. Why have the monkey in? This was a time in the mid-nineteenth century when grown men would talk of having a monkey on the side of one parent or the other – or in Huxley's case, a bulldog, barking for 'Prizes! Pfizer!' For the transhuman with hands and wings. The 'great puzzle' of Alice's identity is that of the arboretum at Pencarrow in Cornwall. Sir William Molesworth, the owner, shows off a latest addition to his arboretum, a Chilean Pine, Alice? to his house party. The barrister and wit, Charles Austin thought it would be a puzzle for a monkey to climb. Alice has only a thimble for herself, her prize for coming equal first. An award to ward off a medical establishment? Or perhaps 'I'm bled,' the colour red of a bottle with the label 'DRINK ME' on… Tenniel coloured in all his illustrations for *The Nursery Alice*, for five-year olds and less. He was blind in one eye and Carroll deaf in one ear, nearing the end of life. Tenniel was meant to draw one – an opera-glass – for the guard on the train Alice finds herself on in chapter three of Book Two, *Through The Looking-glass*. He has the guard look through a pair of visually satisfying binoculars.

OPERA-GLASS
OPEAR-G-LASS

THE PLAGUE DOCTOR

LOOKING-GLASS
ROOK KING-LASS

The two Tweedles' concern that should Alice wake the Red King from his dream of them, their world it would go out… The letter 'g' is coded for omission in the play. That is for another chapter. Minus 'g'…

'I can almost think I can remember feeling a little different. But if I'm not the same, the next question is, Who in the world am I? Ah, that's *the great puzzle.'*

G-REAT MON-*CLE* PUZZLE, TREACLE…

The treacle the dormouse says makes you very ill.

Four

Both Alice books have the same number of chapters, twelve apiece. The corresponding one, chapter to 'A Mad Tea-Party' in Book One, sees Hatta with a change of spelling, not hat, newly released from prison in the chapter seven of Book Two, 'The Lion and the Unicorn'.

They placed themselves close to where Hatta, the other Messenger, was standing watching the fight, with a cup of tea in one hand and a piece of bread and butter in the other.
  'He's only just out of prison, and he hadn't finished his tea when he was sent in,' Haigha whispered to Alice.

A piece, two words... Hatta in chapter five, 'Wool and Water,' of Book Two was in prison for a crime he has yet to commit. Something to do with the way time works on the other side of the glass. Haigha looks a lot like the March Hare...

HATTA, HATTER, TEA-PARTY, HA[TT]ER, HARE...

⋄§ THE PLAGUE DOCTOR §⋄

The White Queen in chapter five justified Hatta's sentencing ahead of time. In chapter seven the White King explains over and over to a puzzled Alice why he must have two messengers, one to come and one to go; one to fetch and one to carry. In other words, they jointly perform the roles of Ariel in the play, Act Four.

PROSPERO *[to Ariel]*   *Ay, with a twink.*

ARIEL
Before you can say, 'come' and 'go',
And breathe twice and cry 'so, so',
Each one tripping on his toe.
Will be here with mop and mow.
Do you love me, master? No?

He does 'dearly, my delicate Ariel'. Now for the White King in chapter seven of Book Two.

'The other Messenger's called Hatta. I must have two you know – to come and go. One to come, and one to go.'
   'I beg your pardon?' said Alice.
   'It isn't respectable to beg,' said the King.
   'I only meant that I didn't understand,' said Alice. 'Why one to come and one to go?'
   'Don't I tell you?' The King repeated patiently. 'I must have two – to fetch and carry. One to fetch and one to carry.'
   At this moment the Messenger arrived; he was far too much

THE PLAGUE DOCTOR

out of breath to say a word, and could only wave his hands about, and make the most fearful faces at the poor King.

'This young lady loves you with an H,' the King said, introducing Alice in the hope of turning off the Messenger's attention from himself – but it was no use – the Anglo-Saxon attitudes only got more extraordinary every moment, while the great eyes rolled wildly from side to side.

'You alarm me!' said the King, 'I feel faint – Give me a ham sandwich!'

Alarm, one word... The Messenger Haigha begins in the chapter as the 'nobody' Alice doesn't see. So Haigha starts life as 'Personne,' and then in adopting the attitudes of Emma Hamillton in Naples, he is something else again, and, if Alice finds Haigha to be hideous – not necessarily like the Hydra – Haigha will lose his H.

'I love my love with an H,' Alice couldn't help beginning, 'because he is Happy. I hate him with an H, because he is Hideous...'

Hideous not Hydeous, no... The problem arises that if the two messengers – sengers, not *singe* – are said to be inseparable – together they perform functions one of Ariel does on her own – then if Haigha loses his H so will Hatta, becoming 'Atta?' Yes. So Haigha gives the White King a ham sandwich with ham, by definition, in the middle in between two pieces of bread. So we know this much about Hatta:

❧ THE PLAGUE DOCTOR ☙

___ ham ___ Atta

Does this ham actor ring a bell? Why would he be in prison for a crime he has yet to commit? A crime of passion or what? The word, mow, it means 'grimace,' Caliban says it of his spirits, Prospero's... Piri? Which is the genitive case of *pirum*, a pear... C-Hatter-at? Do hiss me into madness, -med... he bid 'em?

MOW-HAM-MED ATTA

Mohamed Atta? The face of nine *once*... in prison for a crime he has yet to commit. Ariel can hardly be jailed for a tempest that proves to be illusory. Which or Witch is it? Pears in Latin, *pira*?

PEARSON, *PIRA*CON-C, CONSPIRACY THEORY...

What is it Prospero shall know what I have done *So, King, go safely on to seek thy son*? Ferdinand or Caliban whose speech is next? Ariel has woken Gonzalo just as Sebastian [brother to the king of Naples, Alonso] and usurper Antonio were about to kill both king and councillor.

ARIEL [*to Gonzalo, councillor*]
 My master through his art foresees the danger
 That you, his friend, are in, and sends me forth
 [For else his project dies] to keep them living.
                    Sings in Gonzalo's ear.

THE PLAGUE DOCTOR

While you here do snoring lie,
Open-eyed conspiracy
His time doth take.
If of life you keep a care,
Shake off slumber and beware.
Awake, awake!

Making a conspiracy theory more true than William Shapespeare, an actor who bravely fronts the plays. Ah, with a twink? Ham sandwich or hay, the choice of food for the White King. In chapter seven of Book One, yes at the mad tea-party, the Hatter tells how at the great concert given by the Queen of Hearts...

I had to sing:
   Twinkle, twinkle, little bat!
   How I wonder what you're at!

What if the Queen of Hearts, she's hideous?

H-EARTS, *RATES*...

French ones... *Le bat, la batte, le chauve-souris*... bald mouse, a blind one in Spain... There'd been a rat-hole in chapter one, 'Down the Rabbit-Hole,' of Book One. Re-at-cle? Tweedledum and -dee were about to fight a battle in chapter four of Book Two ...-*kle* Li-bat-tle...

THE PLAGUE DOCTOR

Tweedledum and Tweedledee
Agreed to have a battle;
For Tweedledum said Tweedledee
Had spoiled his nice new rattle.

Just then flew down a monstrous crow,
As black as a tar-barrel;
Which frightened both the heroes so,
They quite forgot their quarrel.

Dum and Dee, Leda's twins? Alice, who has already been mistaken for a snake by a nesting pigeon, tries to break things up.

'Do you see that?' he [Tweedledum] said in a voice choking with passion, and his eyes grew large and yellow all in a moment, as he pointed with a trembling finger at a small white thing lying under the tree.

   'It's only a rattle,' Alice said, after a careful examination of the little white thing. 'Not a rattlesnake, you know,' she added hastily, thinking that he was frightened: 'only an old rattle—quite old and broken.'

   'I knew it was!' cried Tweedledum, beginning to stamp about wildly and tear his hair. 'It's spoilt, of course!' Here he looked at Tweedledee, who immediately sat down on the ground, and tried to hide himself under the umbrella.

RATTLE-C, T-PARTY, TREACLE... MAR[G]ARET-*CLE*-NAN....

Five

Why the yellow eyes? You tell me. What were they talking about? Sebastian and Antonio, before Ariel woke Gonzalo and he woke Alonso? Drowsiness or drowsingeness is it?

Enter *ARIEL* playing solemn music.

SEBASTIAN   *We would so, and then go a bat-fowling.*

ANTONIO [to Gonzalo]   *Nay, good my lord, be not angry.*

GONZALO   *No, I warrant you, I will not adventure my*
  discretion so weakly. Will you laugh me asleep,
  for I am very heavy.

ANTONIO   *Go sleep, and hear us.*
  [All sleep except Alonso, Sebastian and Antonio.]

ALONSO
  What, all so soon asleep? I wish mine eyes
  Would, with themselves, shut up my thoughts. I find
  They are inclined to do so.

THE PLAGUE DOCTOR

SEBASTIAN   *Please you, sir,*
   Do not omit the heavy offer of it.
   It seldom visits sorrow; when it doth,
   It is a comforter.

ANTONIO   *We two, my lord,*
   Will guard your person while you take your rest,
   And watch your safety.

ALONSO   *Thank you. Wondrous heavy.*

[Alonso sleeps. Exit Ariel.]

SEBASTIAN
   What a strange drowsiness possesses them!

ANTONIO
   It is the quality o'th' climate.

SEBASTIAN   *Why*
   Doth it not then our eyelids sink? I find
   Not myself disposed to sleep.

ANTONIO   *Nor I. My spirits are nimble.*
   They fell together all, as by consent.
   They dropped as by a thunderstroke. What might,
   Worthy Sebastian, O, what might—? No more.
   And yet, methinks I see it in your face

THE PLAGUE DOCTOR

What thou shouldst be. Th'occasion speaks thee, and
My strong imagination sees a crown
Dropping upon thy head.

SEBASTIAN   *What, art thou waking?*

ANTONIO
   Do you not hear me speak?

SEBASTIAN   *I do, and surely*
   It is a sleepy language, and thou speak'st
   Out of thy sleep. What is it thou didst say?
   This is a strange repose, to be asleep
   With eyes wide open — standing, speaking, moving —
   And yet so fast asleep.

Antonio, the usurping duke of Milan, Prospero's younger brother, prompts Sebastian, who is the younger brother of Alonso, king of Naples, to do the same, to usurp not a dukedom, a duchy, but the throne of Naples, and to do so not by having Alonso drown at sea, but running him through asleep. Antonio and Sebastian will be on the point of killing Alonso and 'an honest old councillor' Gonzalo when Ariel wakes the latter man who wakes the king, Alonso. What are they planning for the wider community at the same time, for the unwoke, globally?

ANTONIO   *It is the quality of the climate.*

THE PLAGUE DOCTOR

[A Spanish c-inquisition, so *calidad* for quality.]

ANTONIO   *It is the calidad of the climate.*

[Cali?... supercalifragilisticexpialidocious? Cali is Caliban, of course. And who is Dad in the family tree, a Hydra's?

PROSPERO
  ...And Prospero the prime duke, being so reputed.]

ANTONIO   *It is the cali-prime of the climate.*

[The letter 'c' is unseen in on[c]e, and 'l' changes to 'r'.]

CALI-PRIME... PRIMATE [CHANGE].

Change or regression... The means? Treacle, that makes you very ill.

1968: 2001: A Space Odyssey
1971: A Clockwork Orange
1999: Eyes Wide Shut

Films by Stanley Kubrick. Who or what sleeps with eyes open? Is it a reptile? Close...

To be asleep with eyes wide open – standing, speaking, moving – and yet so fast asleep.

THE PLAGUE DOCTOR

To be or not to be. Ariel saves the day, from the night. Why whisper in the ear of Councillor Gonzalo and not the President of America, JFK? The conspiracy theory to begin all conspiracy theories... The confessional? It was to be left on the cover of *Time* magazine, in 1999.

Six

WIKIPEDIA

Batman and his partner, Robin, encounter a new villain, Mr. Freeze, who has left a string of diamond thefts in his wake. During a confrontation at the natural history museum, Freeze steals a large diamond and flees, freezing Robin and leaving Batman unable to pursue him. Later, Batman and Robin learn that Freeze was originally Doctor Victor Fries, a scientist working to develop a cure for a disease known as MacGregor's syndrome, hoping to heal his terminally ill wife, Nora. After a lab accident, Fries was rendered unable to live at average temperatures and forced to wear a cryogenic suit powered by diamonds for survival.

At a Wayne Enterprises lab in Brazil, botanist Doctor Pamela Isley is working under the deranged Doctor Jason Woodrue, who has turned her research on plants into the supersoldier drug Venom. After witnessing Woodrue use the formula to turn serial killer Antonio Diego into the hulking Bane, she threatens to expose Woodrue's experiments. Woodrue attempts to kill her by overturning a shelf of various toxins; instead, Isley is mutated by the toxins into Poison Ivy, who kills Woodrue with a poisonous kiss...

⋅§ THE PLAGUE DOCTOR §⋅

Knowledge of the Little Ice Age to come? Bats happened to be one of three charms – toads, beetles, bats – attributed to his mother Sycorax by Caliban in this conversation with the magician Prospero.

CALIBAN
 ... *Cursed be that I did so! All the charms*
   Of Sycorax – toads, beetles, bats – light on you,
   For I am all the subjects that you have,
   Which first was mine own king; and here you sty me
   In this hard rock...

Another look at the rock and a hard place later on... After a laboratory incident, Uma Thurman has the lethal kiss of a rattlesnake; she is half human, half plant... she is Poison Ivy.

1997   BATMAN AND ROBIN
1998   THE AVENGERS
1999   THE NINTH GATE
1999   EYES WIDE SHUT

Your modus operandi – the way you go about your nefarious activities – is to let your victim know what is in store for him. Why? For the reason of karma? Or that, without agreement of the masses – who consciously do not agree with anything, but are being collectively led like lemmings and have not yet said 'no' to what is planned – without a passive acquiesence to the events you have in mind for the 'useless eaters', they'll

THE PLAGUE DOCTOR

not see the light of day, be staged. Your playbook it's the play *The Tempest*, your pest is Covid, Corvids, Sycorax, Coventry, that go-to-location on the bucket list of the unreformed Nazi. For it to work, for Poison Ivy to step into the role of the ivy in the play, no one – none of your victims – should know that, in addition to adders – some-temps am I all wound with adders, Caliban is – there is a Hydra in the play, that has gone unseen, unnoticed for four hundred years and counting. If Poison Ivy steps into the role of the 'ivy which' in the play, in the film of *The Avengers* in 1998, people might think it odd, later on they would, when this professor Floyd 'Ski' Chilton in Arizona goes public with his discovery of a rattlesnake-like enzyme in those dying of Covid. It took me a while to work out that the Liddell family – Dean Liddell at Christ Church, Oxford, and daughters, Alice among them – is a distraction from what Carroll is about. It took me some time, many months in fact, to realise that her adventures in Wonderland derive or are a riff off *The Tempest*. Then I find, not being a film buff, that the bad actors had made it easier for us humans, they'd made a film in which both Alice and the play are worked in... Still, they must be confident that no one will spot the Hydra, immortal – self-replicating – under the rock in Act One, not after four hundred years of failure to do so... confident enough to have the cinema-goer make it the connection between play and book, a book still not decoded in a century and a half. Who stole the tarts? Treacle tarts. Who? I've just given you the answer: the tarts are the severed necks of the Hydra, stumps of one doubled, like

THE PLAGUE DOCTOR

nanotechnology in the body – injected or breathed in, drunk in – that replicates in the grave, still, in bodies that respond to their MAC-addresses. If the response to Covid is rehearsed, so to advice that now is a good time, would be to give up smoking. The side effects of the Covid injection, or its intended effects, were hid from the public. Peer-reviewed papers on the ill-effects on the body of electromagnetic radiation are never addressed, yet, smoking, that is to be banned, because it blocks the 'nicotine receptor site' on the surface of a cell, that is used by venom in gaining access, hacking it. Did John Tenniel in colouring in the bottle labelled DRINK ME think it odd to have blood-coloured tarts in the one book. Chapter Two of Book One has 'The Pool of Tears' for a title. Fears or rates or treacle… One can see the appeal to a Nazi, to the brother of the left-hand path, of the salute Alice is giving in this illustration for 'The Pool of Tears' … The long tail of this mouse or rat looks to be serpentine… This Orange Teddy Bear in the film made of the 60s UK Cult TV series [The Avengers] is giving a Nazi salute – in pointing up from an external lift on the Lloyds Insurance Building in London, to the avenger on the roof. An incongruous set in that a marble hall from Syon House in South London, with its statue of the Dying Gaul, is somehow built into a Lloyds Building in the City of London. Uma Thurman, she lives on set in a Rogers house, the double house owned by the late Lord Rogers, the Lloyds Building architect. She lives across the Royal Avenue from the Stokers on St Leonards Terrace. It is while at the Rogers' house she receives a call from the

✺ THE PLAGUE DOCTOR ✻

Ministry, that she is to meet John Steed at his club – if not with it, Hercules' – where she finds actor Ralph Fiennes in the nude reading the news, with fur on his chest, a patch of it – he is not yet regressed to a fully furry man. Furman. My guess is – though she herself is the innocent abroad - she will have German blood in her. The eye for detail. An academic with her microscope – it uses 'echo' to build up a 3-D picture of human blood – could see 'a sidewinder', it's a snake in miniature in a human. A mini-rattlesnake? Uma plays Emma Peel and Steed is played by this actor, Ralph Fiennes.

G-RARPH-FIENNES, GRAPHENE IN THE VACCINE...

We're talking control of the birth portals here, recycling. Uma Thurman, The Club Dumas? The title of the book in use for scripting the film of *The Ninth Gate*. Polanski's...

Chapter XI. 'The Banks Of The Seine', The Club Dumas
'I'm not so sure.' She [the former Nazi] tapped the engraving lightly. 'The hermit in the tarot, very similar to this one, is sometimes accompanied by a snake or by a stick that symbolizes it. In occult philosophy, the serpent and the dragon are the guardians of the wonderful enclosure, garden, or fleece, and they sleep with their eyes open. They are the Mirror of the Art.'

It may be worth comparing the snake on the frontispiece of *The Ninth Gate* to that on the armband of Mr Connery in *The Avengers*, to who? Congery in his younger cloning days,

THE PLAGUE DOCTOR

hence his offer to Father to double the Bet in their game of croquet. The winning stick looks to be the spike protein, ersatz. As Sean's red ball strikes it, we cut to his henchman Eddie Izzard in his Mini Coupe? Is it from the Ministry? Not Bill Lizard in Wonderland, no so we cut to 'Bailey', with the ball now a flat disc on his lap. Multiple levers are to control this swarm of bees, or wasps, that aerosolise the sky, the humans below. Who plays Alice? One moment... Eileen Atkins. If Atta is left unsaid so too the wasp episode was omitted, because John Tenniel is unable to come up with an illustration that goes with it. So the hedgehog, Alice's, is the spike protein. Evidence of injection in the upper arm? Under the arm patch of Connery, the geoengineer, no, but he does dart two of his scientists – Babbington and Morton – inject them in the upper arm in 1998... Dead, not dying like the Gaul. Instant, both, they'd failed the loyalty test. Their scene in a marble room at Syon House is filmed at a time the shadows of statues look to oversee their 'ritual' killing. Sean, without his Teddy head on, looks cryptid like the throwback in man's past to an oversized hominid – if it is not him standing in for Hercules... No lion's mane to go over his shoulders... He sells weather in Greenwich Palace. There's talk of it being our winter of discontent ... Thinking of lions, Antonio, Horatio... Furman she has been trying to get Fiennes to eat a grape, graphene and failing to do so, this until she has him in check in chess. Czech Mate, Prague, Plague, maybe not, not yet, when he drinks a glass of red wine. A third connection to the late Lord Rogers would be

❧ THE PLAGUE DOCTOR ☙

the proposed extension, his to the National Gallery, yes, in Trafalgar Square. Prince Charles as he then was, thought it to be a carbuncle, a 'monstrous carbuncle,' the monster Caliban... Horatio Nelson, who, like the ravens at the Tower of London... like yes Shakespeare, symbolise our sovereign nation, has been knocked off his column [made of Dartmoor granite] by blind 'Father' in the Wonderland Weather balloon. Admiral Hardy, Hydra?, has kissed the dying Nelson on his way, once at his Nelson's request, then again on seeing the hero blind drowning in his blood. Uma Thurman – if I say her, Emma Peel, you will think of Emma Booker at her Elementary School in Florida – kisses Steed, Fiennes, her 'Prince Charming' twice. In the final scene on a roof in Whitehall overlooking the Thames, Jim Broadbent as 'Mother', toasts a job well done. The champagne?... Piper Heidsieck. A raven in the distance, a last one?, flies away from the Tower. Prince Charming? Fiennes, a clone of his former self.

Seven

John Steed, a man-horse, a centaur... or Hercules with a centaur's poisoned blood running in him?

[The centaur] Nessus felt that the poison would soon kill him, and he longed to revenge himself on Heracles by doing him some injury. So he said to Deianira, 'Take a cloth and dip it in my blood, and do not let Heracles see it; but if ever you are afraid that he loves another woman better than you, sprinkle the blood over his clothing, and he will be unable to leave you. You must take care, however, not to touch it yourself.'

Heracles, Roman Hercules, had dipped his arrows in the blood of the Hydra and killed Nessus with one of them, for carrying Deianira off on his back.

Deianira was greatly afraid that Heracles might forsake her for the beautiful Iole whom he had formerly wished to marry, and remembering what the Centaur had told her to do if ever she had any special reason for desiring that Heracles be true to her, she took the cloth which had been soaked in his blood, and

THE PLAGUE DOCTOR

smeared all the inner side of the robe with it. Lichas took the robe to Heracles, and he put it on. But when the blood had become warmed by the heat of his body, it burst into flames and burnt Heracles so terribly that in his agony he seized Lichas by the feet and flung him three times against the rocks, till his face was all battered, and none of the features could be distinguished. Then he tried to tear off the dress, but it clung so closely to his skin that pieces of his flesh came off with it. He suffered unspeakable tortures, which made him cry out with the pain and roll on the ground in agony, and then he moaned piteously that the very stones might have felt for him, but no one dared go near him. For a short time the pain made him quite mad...

... and not for the first time. He'd also worn a dress before as a transvestite in the court of a queen. He resolves to burn himself to death on a funeral pyre, but can find no one to light it, till a herdsman was persuaded by the offer of Heracles' bow and arrows.

The wind fanned the flames and they mounted higher and higher, but before they reached Heracles himself, a sound of thunder and lightning was heard, and a cloud came down which covered the funeral pile and in which he was carried up to the top of Mount Olympus. The gods gifted him with immortality as a recompense for his noble deeds, and they said that he should henceforth be as one of themselves. Even Hera did not grudge him his reward, for her hatred had at last been conquered by his great and godlike Labours.

THE PLAGUE DOCTOR

With the addition of blood from the Hydra and the centaur Nessus, the transhuman Hercules achieves immortality through his labour. From a translation by Frances Younghusband of the German original, Professor C. Witt's *Myths Of Hellas*. With his back to the Dying Gaul in the marble hall at Syon House, this headless Teddy Bear – Connery or Conger Eel - is part-Teddy man and divine. A black silver-back, he runs Wonderland Weather. Fiennes tells Uma Furman in the Bentley, Sir Sean aka Sir August de Wynter, a blackmailing geoengineer, he'd left the Ministry under something of a cloud. One of the four black lions at Nelson's Column is shot so as to look like some brooding giant, Hercules with his lion's skin. Like Caliban who never yields us kind answer, yes, or like Eileen Atkins. Not just playwright G. Bernard Shaw who would hire his actors by name or have them come through the birth portal on time... Jim Broadbent talks to the Prime Minister, Blair, on the phone. The Weather Shield is down... R. Shield for short. You'd have to have a President to go with Pearson. Try Treason. And then you need someone for Wheelers Family Butchery, yes, leaving the Michelin Man at Abbots Motor Services. L to R. No names for the black and white men, mechanics, with their monkey wrenches. No, Nicholas Woodeson is the time-keeper at Steed's obstacle course in which he disarms a police constable with a club, before meeting Uma Furman at his London club, Boodles. Yes, a small world, if you are of Hercules' build. Not just Prospero who uses the word, Prime, no, Ferdinand has a prime request

THE PLAGUE DOCTOR

to make of Miranda, to know 'if you be maid or no?' She looks to be one half mRNA. Was Patrick Macnee chosen as Steed for his acting back in the 60s? Now working in Archives and invisible, he has his replacement, Fiennes, talk to his pipe. How would that go with Piper Heidsieck and which of Fiennes is it? The mechanical clone having his first or last kiss in Trafalgar Square or the one with the pink carnation. Car-nation, not Bizet, no. No temps, not counting Secretary Henry Maynard. The Prime Minister of Canada, Carney, premature. I do not mean by it, he needs to hang for a bit, no.

Eight

'At the first sight they have changed eyes.'

Miranda and Ferdinand have... The observation, it is Prospero's own, made to Ariel, if Ariel is not running the show, a one-woman show? Changed eyes, fallen in love at first sight, or changed identities one for the other...

Hasn't it got pretty pink eyes [I think all *White Rabbits have pink eyes]; and pink ears; and a nice brown coat; and you can just see its red pocket-handkerchief peeping out of its coat-pocket: and, what with its blue neck-tie and its yellow waistcoat, it really is* very *nicely dressed.*

   'Oh dear, oh dear!' said the Rabbit. 'I shall be too late!' What would it be too late for*, I wonder? Well, you see, it had to go and visit the Duchess [you'll see a picture of the Duchess, soon, sitting in the kitchen]: and the Duchess was a very cross old lady: and the Rabbit knew* she'd *be very angry indeed if he kept her waiting. So the poor thing was as frightened as frightened could be [Don't you see how he's trembling? Just shake the book a little, from side to side...]*

THE PLAGUE DOCTOR

An albino with pink eyes? I th-ink k-all, Caliban, Carbon... Two late four... for a readership of 'children aged from nought to five,' per the preface to *The Nursery Alice* published in 1890 'containing twenty coloured enlargements from Tenniel's Illustrations...' Now we know what colour the drink is in the bottle, blood red – pram red – and the bow in the bonnet of the Duchess' cook, butterfly blue. From mushroom to a pillar, shackled to it in chapter five 'Wool and Water' of Book Two. Laine, Raine? Alice's left hand in the kitchen is held at the same angle as the cook's only she has no pepper in it. The duchess, her looks are those of an old woman painted c.1500 by Quentin Massy: she was Margaretha 'Maultasch', thought to be.

CARBON CREDIT, CLE-*SAID*...
MISS HAVISHAMPIGNON, POORKING, HAMLET...
P-INK EYES, EN[C]RE... LATE, RATE, H-*ENRETARD*...
P-ILL-AR, LIAR, *10/6*...

Rotate hat to *9[o]11*, from Knight's move up pillar.

MIRANDA   *The strangeness of your story out*
   Heaviness in me.

PROSPERO   *Shake it off. Come on,*
   We'll visit Caliban, my slave, who never
   Yields us kind answer.

THE PLAGUE DOCTOR

Eileen Atkins, with her pram, two knives, a screaming child, no longer on her way to Wheelers Family Butchery. Michelin man, eel-like... 'Check your tyre pressures'? Tyre and Sidon plessures at Abbots, 3 miles from Lambury... Kit off?

RABBIT-HOLE, RAT-HOLE, RATTLESNAKE, TREACLE WELL... RABBI TEA-PARTY, DIS-RAELI... I'M LATE, ON THE VERGE...

The author of *The Gardener Who Saw God*, Edward James of West Dean, Sussex, a surrealist and the natural son or grandson of a king, patronised Salvador Dali. He gave him a stuffed Polar Bear that was to go in his hall, beside Dali's copy of Giorgione's 'Tempest', at Port Lligat. James, being a surrealist – who could only see the back of his head in his mirror, Magritte's – had had the bear dyed purple. In all likelihood, James it was who filled in Dali and Dali his other patron [the pharmaceuticals heir, Sandoz, Cheshire] re. Tudor history: who the bard is really... The Tempest was real enough; it had deposited at what would have been Dali's doorstep, an incorruptible body in the charge of the young Philip II of Spain, 'Bloody Mary', her husband, de jure uxoris future king of England. Sandoz runs with the information: in his book *The Maze* he has a 175-year-old toad at the remote Craven Castle in Scotland and in his *On The Verge* [opera-glass?] he sails too close to the wind. He even – by the book's end – anticipates his own in the White Villa, an asylum in North Africa, but also his villa on his island off Naples, another white one... David Garrick, the famous

THE PLAGUE DOCTOR

Shakespearean actor of his day, in the chapter after the one titled 'MR. RABBI', gives Sandoz, his visitor at the asylum, an account of how he ended up there mad. This third unnumbered chapter of *On The Verge* has 'TRAP' for a title, PART backward, RAT, Desert Rat? Anyway, the book's narrator, Sandoz – is he writing this while in his White Villa? – meets Major Garrick in Belvedere Park in Tunis. Inmates at the nearby asylum, White Villa, get to spend time in De Vere's park on good behaviour. Herve de Grandsailles in Dali's one novel *Hidden Faces* is going to be Versailles de Vere, as an aside. He, it was, who'd polish up the dinner conversation of his notaire, Pierre Girardin, passing it off as his own work, that of the Comte de Grandsailles, when in Paris society.

My comrade, Major Lawrence Green, had just been dispatched, bearing a sealed message, to the Oasis of Nefta ... He never came back.

Olivier? U not W... *I Vier*, four? I had not thought of that, of *once* being eleven to a Spaniard. Ring, *sonne*... not a red message a sealed one.

I was in despair at his disappearance, which I felt sure was due to a tragedy...

By following in his footsteps Major Garrick hopes to find out what became of his friend and fellow radio operator, Vert. So place names will be all-important.

THE PLAGUE DOCTOR

Having dressed myself [to] look like a commericial traveller in oil and soap, and provided myself with a small suitcase full of scented samples, which concealed the code message beneath, I set out on my journey. At Susa I easily found the hotel where my friend had passed the night; his name appeared in the hotel register. At Sfax I found the same. At Tozeur the French military attaché assured me that he had shaken hands with Lawrence three weeks before. Finally, at Nefta, the blind host of the only inn of the oasis told me that Lawrence had arrived at midnight two weeks earlier and had left at five o'clock in the morning for an unknown destination. I knew what this unknown destination was, for I was carrying a sealed message which was a duplicate of the one which had never been delivered.

In the fourth of these unnumbered chapters, not counting the Preface, Maurice Sandoz is back at the White Villa; he is to catch up with a demoted Lieutenant Garrick, but bumps instead into a man called of all names, Olivier, whom Dr Fournier had allocated to the room next to Garrick's, who was to keep an eye on him – for he has a violent past.

I entered Georges Olivier's room and held out his cigarette.
  'Was it you who bombarded me with this curious projectile?'
  'You must admit that it's harmless,' Olivier replied with a broad smile, 'and very much less dangerous than the tin sword that glittered in my suit of armor when I was a little boy. Not a very good little boy either, for at this early age I was, as you see, a soldier at heart. I have long since past that stage, I can assure you.'

THE PLAGUE DOCTOR

Bombarde? One word… At about this time Olivier is playing Henry V in the film of the play, to bolster troop morale. 'Why all this mystery?' A frustrated Sandoz, who is trying to have Olivier freed as sane after all, asks him. He would keep Olivier informed of his attempt to have him freed…

That was as far as I could get. An atrocious pain cut short my breath … I had time to see the distorted, almost unrecognizable features of Olivier the madman bent over me, and his strong hands holding an iron bar [no doubt wrenched from its sockets in the window] digging in my side.

He loses consciousness, Sandoz does. Dr Fournier is nearly too late. He cannot free Sandoz because it would reveal low staffing levels at the asylum: Fournier is running the White Villa on the cheap, a shoe-string budget, and pocketing the difference. Recognize, to recognize, is a verb he, Sandoz, uses in his book *The Maze*. Are we talking conger eels? He has just told us that the scale had diminished?

Nine

From Bill Lizard in his Mini Coupe to a suspected outbreak, make that case, a case of cooping – when someone is sent in to vote, before being dressed in another's clothing then sent in to vote again, when he has no interest in polling, in politics... Edgar Allan Poe is found face down in the gutter dressed in someone else's clothes outside a polling station in Baltimore, when he is meant to be in New York. He was said to be delirious and died in hospital having cried out a name, 'Reynolds!' more than once... Was he the Reynolds who espoused a Hollow Earth Theory, Jeremiah Reynolds, who might be supposed to have got 'Arthur Gordon Pym of Nantucket' right to the entrance at the South Pole and no further in Poe's single attempt at writing a novel? Did he mistake the tunnel one sees at death for the way into the Earth at the South Pole? An aside: Tenniel illustrated Bill leaving via the chimney. The adjacent chimney pot it has a cowl on, leaving the reader with the impression of there being two plumes of smoke rising from a severed, serpentine neck. Two for one neck cut but not cauterised. The Hydra's. Poe writes of the Conqueror Worm at death in his account of it

THE PLAGUE DOCTOR

with an advisor cat on his shoulder and his Aunt Clemm keeping him company, knitting into a long night. Long too for his young wife coughing blood into the small hours. If there were two of Fiennes, one who picked a white carnation and the other the pink, could there be a Poe with a pink buttonhole – the one found in the gutter? Was there another reason why he had to die that night? Was he sentenced because of one of his own sentences? Poe cracked the code of *The Tempest*; he writes it out in his 1845 poem *The Raven* when he is not peering deep into the darkness.

CORVUS CORAX, SYCORATHENE...

He has a bust of Pallas, which is a bust of Athene, and has a raven sit on it. Verse seven of eighteen.

*Open here I flung the shutter, when, with many a flirt and
    flutter,
In there stepped a stately Raven of the saintly days of yore;
Not the least obeisance made he; not a minute stopped or
    stayed he;
But, with mien of lord or lady, perched above my chamber
door— Perched upon a bust of Pallas just above my chamber
door— Perched, and sat, and nothing more.*

There is a tempest, too. Verse fifteen.

"Prophet!" said I, "thing of evil!—prophet still, if bird or devil!—

THE PLAGUE DOCTOR

*Whether Tempter sent, or whether tempest tossed thee here
   ashore,
Desolate yet all undaunted, on this desert land enchanted—
On this home by Horror haunted—tell me truly, I implore—
Is there—is there balm in Gilead?—tell me—tell me, I implore!"
Quoth the Raven "Nevermore."*

STAY, NOT YET, STAY, PAS EN[C]ORE, L'ENORE...

Lenore is identified in verse sixteen.

*"Prophet!" said I, "thing of evil!—prophet still, if bird or devil!
By that Heaven that bends above us—by that God we both
   adore—
Tell this soul with sorrow laden if, within the distant Aidenn,
It shall clasp a sainted maiden whom the angels name Lenore—
Clasp a rare and radiant maiden whom the angels name Lenore."
Quoth the Raven "Nevermore."*

Whether on the cat's advice or his own initiative, Poe follows it up with a poem *Lenore* which identifies Guy de Vere in the first of four verses.

*Ah broken is the golden bowl! the spirit flown forever!
Let the bell toll!—a saintly soul floats on the Stygian river;
And, Guy De Vere, hast thou no tear?—weep now or never
   more!
See! on yon drear and rigid bier low lies thy love, Lenore!*

THE PLAGUE DOCTOR

Come! let the burial rite be read—the funeral song be sung!—
An anthem for the queenliest dead that ever died so young—
A dirge for her the doubly dead in that she died so young.

Poe's punished for a crime he has yet to commit, yes, like Hatta after him. Had he given away the coding in the play in 1845, the coding in play in 2001 and 2019, he would have had her, a Queen of Hearts after him.

Ten

Delicate Ariel? Is Ariel her Kate in the song of the play's butler, Stephano, in scene two of Act Two? Caliban has made his 'madness' speech which is interrupted by the jester Trinculo lost on his island. Now Stephano enters:

STEPHANO
    I shall no more to sea, to sea.
    Here shall I die ashore—

This is a very scurvy tune to sing at a man's funeral.
Well, here's my comfort.

                                      Drinks [and then] sings.
    The master, the swabber, the boatswain, and I,
        The gunner and his mate,
    Loved Mall, Meg, and Marian, and Margery,
        But none of us cared for Kate.
    For she had a tongue with a tang,
    Would cry to a sailor "Go hang!"
    She loved not the savour of tar nor of pitch,

THE PLAGUE DOCTOR

Yet a tailor might scratch her where'er she
did itch.
Then to sea, boys, and let her go hang!
This is a scurvy tune too. But here's my comfort.
Drinks.

CALIBAN *Do not torment me! O!*

So to Peg and I Pearl [Ariel?] we have Mall, Meg, and Marian to add. [Miranda, she responds to Ferdinand that she is indeed a maid. The White Rabbit mistakes Alice for his maid, Mary Ann.] Not till Act Four do we have an addition, if she is, of sea-marge [sea-margin] in Iris' speech of greeting to Ceres, Demeter as she is in Greece. The goddesses are embodied on Earth for their blessing of a marriage, Miranda's to Ferdinand.

IRIS
  Ceres, most bounteous lady, thy rich leas
  Of wheat, rye, barley, vetches, oats, and peas;
  Thy turfy mountains, where live nibbling sheep,
  And flat meads thatched with stover, them to keep;
  Thy banks with pionèd and twillèd brims,
  Which spongy April at thy hest betrims
  To make cold nymphs chaste crowns; and thy broomgroves,
  Whose shadow the dismissèd bachelor loves,
  Being lass-lorn; thy pole-clipped vineyard;
  And thy sea-marge, sterile and rocky hard,

THE PLAGUE DOCTOR

Where thou thyself dost air— the Queen o' th' Sky,
Whose watery arch and messenger am I,
Bids thee leave these, and with her sovereign grace,

JUNO descends,
Here on this grass plot, in this very place,
To come and sport. Her peacocks fly amain.
Approach, rich Ceres, her to entertain.

Juno, not Hera, her Greek name.

RICH LEAS, I HERACLES, HERCULES

Thy rich leas being the natural growth of the goddess Ceres, but then so is Proserpina her progeny.

PROSERPINA, SERPENT, MAKE G-APE THE PINE....
I PEARSON, HER-CULES, SULES?

Prospero makes gape the pine or pineal letting Ariel out...

GRASS PLOT, L to R, GLASS PLOT, VERRE? LASS-LORN...
G-LASS-LORN, OPERA-G-LASS...

SEA MARGE, NAN MARGARET STERILE...
ROCKY-HARD, HYDRA...

In the coloured-in edition of Wonderland, Alice sits within a

THE PLAGUE DOCTOR

green armchair that encircles her, next to a tree with green ivy growing round it and the March Hare holds a cup up in front of the constricted tree. Is one meant to read in the colour red for tea-cups?

...and she [Alice] found them having tea under a great tree, with Dormouse sitting between them.

In chapter one, 'Looking-Glass House' of Book Two, Carroll has Alice discover this poem 'Jabberwocky', which is written backward in a looking-glass world. Carroll would seem to be prompting his readers to recall Iris' speech and see how he's writing of Alice with the play of *The Tempest* to hand, Iris in mind.

JABBERWOCKY
'Twas brillig, and the slithy toves
Did gyre and gimble in the wabe:
All mimsy were the borogoves,
And the mome raths outgrabe.

'Beware the Jabberwock, my son!
The jaws that bite, the claws that catch!
Beware the Jubjub bird, and shun
The frumious Bandersnatch!'

He took his vorpal sword in hand;
Long time the manxome foe he sought—

THE PLAGUE DOCTOR

So rested he by the Tumtum tree
  And stood awhile in thought.

And, as in uffish thought he stood,
  The Jabberwock, with eyes of flame,
Came whiffling through the tulgey wood,
  And burbled as it came!

One, two! One, two! And through and through
  The vorpal blade went snicker-snack!
He left it dead, and with its head
  He went galumphing back.

'And hast thou slain the Jabberwock?
  Come to my arms, my beamish boy!
O frabjous day! Callooh! Callay!'
  He chortled in his joy.

'Twas brillig, and the slithy toves
  Did gyre and gimble in the wabe:
All mimsy were the borogoves,
  And the mome raths outgrabe.

So the seventh verse is a repeat of the first. John Tenniel illustrates this 'beamish boy, my son,' as he cuts a head of Hydra off in a forest of necks? Are the bat's wings on the Jabberwock from the umbrella of Tweededum or the hangglider over Isreal, crossing over from Palestine in what is an official film? What fools we – these mortals – be!

❧ THE PLAGUE DOCTOR ☙

G-YRE, RYE, BETRIMS, MIMSY...
BOROGOVES, BROOMFROVES...
NIBBLING, IBBLINNG, GIMBLE...
THATCHED WITH STOVER, TOVES...

By the sixth chapter of *Through The Looking-Glass*, Carroll looks to be having second thoughts; he has Humpty Dumpty give meanings to the words in the poem that do not relate it to the play, *The Tempest*.

'Don't stand chattering to yourself like that...'
 'You seem very clever at explaining words, Sir,' said Alice.
 'Would you kindly tell me the meaning of the poem called "Jabberwocky"?'
 'Let's hear it,' said Humpty Dumpty. 'I can explain all the poems that were ever invented—and a good many that haven't been invented just yet.'
 This sounded very hopeful, so Alice repeated the first verse.
 'That's enough to begin with,' Humpty Dumpty interrupted: 'there are plenty of hard words there. "Brillig" means four o'clock in the afternoon—the time when you begin broiling things for dinner.'
 'That'll do very well,' said Alice: 'and "slithy"?'
 'Well, "slithy" means "lithe and slimy." "Lithe" is the same as "active." You see it's like a portmanteau—there are two meanings packed up into one word.'
 'I see it now,' Alice remarked thoughtfully: 'and what are "toves"?'

'Well, "toves" are something like badgers—they're something like lizards—and they're something like corkscrews.'

'They must be very curious looking creatures.'

'They are that,' said Humpty Dumpty: 'also they make their nests under sun-dials—also they live on cheese.'

'And what's the "gyre" and to "gimble"?'

'To "gyre" is to go round and round like a gyroscope. To "gimble" is to make holes like a gimlet.'

'And "the wabe" is the grass-plot round a sun-dial, I suppose?' said Alice, surprised at her own ingenuity.

'Of course it is. It's called "wabe," you know, because it goes a long way before it, and a long way behind it—'

'And a long way beyond it on each side,' Alice added.

'Exactly so. Well, then, "mimsy" is "flimsy and miserable" (there's another portmanteau for you). And a "borogove" is a thin shabby-looking bird with its feathers sticking out all round—something like a live mop.'

'And then "mome raths"?' said Alice. 'I'm afraid I'm giving you a great deal of trouble.'

'Well, a "rath" is a sort of green pig: but "mome" I'm not certain about. I think it's short for "from home"—meaning that they'd lost their way, you know.'

'And what does "outgrabe" mean?'

'Well, "outgrabing" is something between bellowing and whistling, with a kind of sneeze in the middle: however, you'll hear it done, maybe—down in the wood yonder— and when you've once heard it you'll be quite content. Who's been repeating all that hard stuff to you?'

THE PLAGUE DOCTOR

Ariel? – who has this to sing in the first scene of Act Five:

ARIEL
> *Where the bee sucks, there suck I,*
> *In a cowslip's bell I lie;*
> *There I couch when owls do cry.*
> *On a bat's back I do fly*
> *After summer merrily*
> *Merrily, merrily, shall I live now,*
> *Under the blossom that hangs on the bough.*

One of the other hang-gliders, Hamas', is worth a second look.

Eleven

*'... that now he was the ivy which had hid my
princely trunk and sucked my verdure out on't.
Thou attend'st not!'*

Miranda, she says she is at -X- ding and Prospero then asks her to mark him, with the mark of the beast? Of Caliban...

TEN, F-IVY, C-INQUISITION...
MAIN-TENANT, TEN, FOUR-MI, FIVE...
HAD I NOT FOUR OR FIVE WOMEN ONCE *ONCE*
  THAT TEN...
TEN-DE-DE-TEN, VOUS-AVEZ SOU-VENT...
LA HIEDRA, HAD, HID, LE LIERRE...
W-HAT JE-SUIS-SANS BOTTES...

And we know that by the time Carroll is writing chapter six of Book Two, 'Humpty Dumpty', he suffers from a loss of nerve and tries to undo the impression already given, that Alice is taken – was a riff – from the play of *The Tempest*. How many *pestes*, pestilences? Double 'u', double 'n', a Biblical ten.

THE PLAGUE DOCTOR

If the reserve, Carroll's in writing chapter six, was intended to throw his reader back off the Jabberwock's scent, his chapter three had given the big game away. It has 'Looking-Glass Insects' for a title. Is the elephant caught in a metamorphosis? At the end of chapter two, Alice, knowing that she is a pawn on a chessboard, knows she'll have to move the piece that she is. There is talk of pegs, then the Queen leaves her be. What happens between the end of chapter two and the moment she is told in three to:

CHANGE ENGINES, CHANGE INTO A FRENCH MONKEY... LA-BELLED '[G]LASS WITH CARE', VERRE HERBE HARE?

Alice she was preoccupied in Book One, the start of it, not knowing whether she'd changed as a person, into a *SINGE* puzzle... What will the first *chose* to do in three, given our opening quote from ACT ONE?

CHAPTER THREE: LOOKING-GLASS INSECTS
Of course the first thing to do was to make a grand survey of the country she was going to travel through. 'It's something very like learning geography,' thought Alice, as she stood on tiptoe in hopes of being able to see a little further. 'Principal rivers—there are none. Principal mountains—I'm on the only one, but I don't think it's got any name. Principal towns—why, what are those creatures, making honey down there? They can't be bees — nobody ever saw bees a mile off, you know—' and for some time she stood silent, watching one of them that was bustling about

THE PLAGUE DOCTOR

---

among the flowers, poking its proboscis into them, 'just as if it was a regular bee,' thought Alice.

However, this was anything but a regular bee: in fact it was an elephant—as Alice soon found out, though the idea quite took her breath away at first. 'And what enormous flowers they must be!' was her next idea. 'Something like cottages with the roofs taken off, and stalks put to them—and what quantities of honey they must make! I think I'll go down and—no, I won't just yet,' she went on, checking herself just as she was beginning to run down the hill, and trying to find some excuse for turning shy so suddenly. 'It'll never do to go down among them without a good long branch to brush them away—and what fun it'll be when they ask me how I like my walk. I shall say—"Oh, I like it well enough—"' (here came the favourite little toss of the head), '"only it was so dusty and hot, and the elephants did tease so!"'

'I think I'll go down the other way,' she said after a pause: 'and perhaps I may visit the elephants later on. Besides, I do so want to get into the Third Square!'

So with this excuse she ran down the hill and jumped over the first of the six little brooks.

Little b-rooks, 'Billets, please.' The Guard could just as well be talking to Bill Lizard? I was thinking more of Eddie? No – Miranda...

PRINCELY TRUNK, CONCEALED? PRINCIPAL RIVERS...
BEING ABEL MAGWITCH? LABELLED, ABEILLE, APIARY...
MAYKING HONEY? HONEYSUCKLE [SEE BELOW]...

THE PLAGUE DOCTOR

NOBODY EVER SAW BEES A MIEL OFF, PERSONNE...
TO BE ABLE TO SEE NOBODY, DRAMATIS PERSONAE?
BUSTLING, POKING PROBOSCIS, ELEPHANT TRUNK...
ENORMOUS, GREAT ORME, SEA-SNAKE, ROCKY...
STALKS, DEAD-HEADED FLOWERS...
LITTLE TOSS OF THE HEAD, ONE OF THE HYDRA'S...
SOME EXCUSE FOR TURNING SHY SO SUDDENLY?

The guard on the train she finds herself on looks at her through binoculars, not the opera-glass it should be... Confirmation that the ivy should be thought of as female comes from *A Midsummer Night's Dream*, Titania's speech made to Bottom, the ass in it. She, drugged by Oberon, sees him as her beau.

TITANIA
  I have a venturous fairy that shall seek
  The squirrel's hoard and fetch thee new nuts.

BOTTOM   *I had rather have a handful or two of dried*
  peas. But I pray you, let none of your people stir me.
  I have an exposition of sleep come upon me.

TITANIA
  Sleep thou, and I will wind thee in my arms.
  Fairies, be gone, and be all ways away.

                              Music stops. Exeunt Fairies.

THE PLAGUE DOCTOR

So doth the woodbine the sweet honeysuckle
Gently entwist. The female ivy so
Enrings the barky fingers of the elm.

Orme...

New formed 'em; having both the key of officer and office... Lion? *Loni-cera...* Key *d'or, fourmi.*

Twelve

ADA CLARE, *CLE*...

Ada? The wife of Richard Carstone in the novel *Bleak House*, Dickens'... Dickens, along with Prime Minister Disraeli, his sponsor, together with the author Edward Bulwer, Lord Lytton of Knebworth [who wrote of *The Coming Race*, a subterranean one] are all of them in this 'Orphic Circle' ... Prepubescent girls, the likes of Emma Hardinge, are put into trance, this in order for her to communicate with higher or lower realms is it? Knebworth is a short ride away from Hatfield House, ancestral home of the Cecil descendants of Robert, the younger son of William Cecil, Lord Treasurer. Oxford Don Charles Dodgson, 'Dodo', is a guest, a regular one at Hatfield, where he entertains the younger generation with more of his, Carroll's tall stories. An aside to do with Robert Cecil and Henry Maynard, his secretary bird. Henry and his growing family have been living at Mortlake, where John Dee, who taught ciphers to Francis Bacon, stables Henry's horses and does the horoscope of his latest progeny. The Maynards in an act of humour, of wordplay taken too

THE PLAGUE DOCTOR

far, move to their new manor in Tooting Graveney. [Anyone who watches the film of *The Avengers* would have been thinking along these lines already.] As his Principal Secretary, Henry would not be personally in awe, live in fear of the queen. Yet we would not guess it from a communication of his sent to his boss, employer Robert Cecil.

H. Maynard to Sir Robert Cecil.

1594, Nov. 8. I am scared with a message that hath been sent to me from Clapham by a man of mine that I have left there, that one of the Guard hath been at my house this day to see it, signifying her Majesty's meaning to drive there on Thursday next in her remove hither. If there be any such speech (as I hope there is not) I beseech you be a means to alter that purpose. For I may truly say to you I am not yet certain whether I shall agree for the house or not, the executors of D. Clarke, from whom I have my interest, and those of his widow, being in question about the same. I doubt not, by Lord Cobham's favour, being now the director of these removes as lord Chamberlain, and your good means in such sort as you can best devise the same, but to be rid of this fear. — Strand, 8 November, 1594.

P.S. — I doubt not but my lady will put to her helping hand herein. But if there should be no remedy, I must disclaim from being owner of the house.

From the archives at Hatfield House as is a note sent with

THE PLAGUE DOCTOR

plums – picked by his Henry's own hand – for Robert to eat. We are talking of a time when a game of bowls is finished before the Spanish massing in the Channel are engaged. What was there to hide? What beans might his cornered wife spill to the queen? What did she Susan have to hide? End of aside. Coding of correspondence, books, can be of two sorts, one requiring common sense to decipher, the other – like the communications of the Duke of Wellington - required a decoding manual at the other end. Common sense decoding is just that: you try what's obvious. If a letter can sound like another, then that may be the way forward, a clue. Sometimes the first letter in a word is to be deleted or there is a shift to try, maybe of three letters, from J to M, say. Little tricks of the trade.

JARNDYCE V JARNDYCE

Dickens? He would have known Hatfield House from his youth; he was a correspondent, a journalist who'd cover the fire at Hatfield when an elderly lady's wig got too close to a candle... Dickens on his tour of America, post mortem – that of Poe – gives his Aunt Clemm a fat cheque. Like Carroll – who was known for his extraordinary acts of generosity – Dickens, who knew what a debtor's prison was from the inside, was generous and not to a fault. The odd thing about the chronology of events, the timing of Poe's poem 'The Raven', is that it looks from the outside as though he broke the code, the bootless inquisition on his own, without help

THE PLAGUE DOCTOR

from across the pond. Carroll, of course, wrote for Dickens, his magazine under an assumed name, nom de plum? Plume... They are of course writing at the same time.

GREAT EXPECTATIONS
TREACLE EXPECTATIONS
GREAT REXPECTAIONS

Dickens let it be known that Miss Havisham was in part if not wholly based on a jilted Donnithorne, a Cornish girl at first sight, yes ostensibly. Only she was not. He had met in Twickenham, Eliza Donnithorne's family, learning from them of their descent from a Spaniard, shipwrecked one. Dickens wrote without a feline on his shoulder, often on his feet as if channeling voices spoken on the astral plane, bringing them down to Earth within hearing range, with all the attendant copyright problems. Someone contacts you. They have found out a family member of yours knows Lausanne in Switzerland and wants you to do them a literary favour. Dickens knows by then – the death of his talkative raven Grip – that what he sends his illustrator – Grip's obituary – will be kept for posterity by his illustrator Daniel Maclise, were his own copy of it, his letter, to ever be lost. He tells Maclise that Grip dies of a medicinal overdose of Castor Oil and drops another hint – other than Roil – in coding it, the obituary. Not to do with a-belle witch, that is not directly, no... Estella, L to R, a slap, you've lost me. I've lost my place, thread, all of it. Little Philip?

THE PLAGUE DOCTOR

PHILIP PIP PIRGRIP...

I shall resort, because I have to, to Sonnet 18, to make up the shortfall in words, this chapter, before moving on to the Morlocks? No, not New York, to Daisy... not the pawn in Book Two, Daisy Maynard.

SONNET 18
Shall I compare thee to a summer's day?
Thou art more lovely and more temperate:
Rough winds do shake the darling buds of May,
And summer's lease hath all too short a date;
Sometime too hot the eye of heaven shines,
And often is his gold complexion dimm'd;
And every fair from fair sometime declines,
By chance or nature's changing course untrimm'd;
But thy eternal summer shall not fade,
Nor lose possession of that fair thou ow'st;
Nor shall death brag thou wander'st in his shade,
When in eternal lines to time thou grow'st:
   So long as men can breathe or eyes can see,
   So long lives this, and this gives life to thee.

SHALL I COMPARE, I SHALL PARECOM...
THOU ART MORE TEMPERATE, PEARTE?
ROUGH WINDS, ASPEROUGH...
THE DARRING BUDS OF MAY?
COMPLEXION, COMPLEXI[C]ON?
AND EVERY FAIR, DE VERE....

Thirteen

'There was a table set out under the tree in front of the house, and the March Hare and the Hatter were having tea at it...'

'Your hair wants cutting,' said the Hatter. He had been looking at Alice for some time with great curiosity...

Your hair or Hare wants?... Mini-*coupe*...

'Who in the world am I? Ah, that's *the great puzzle!*'

Who in the world am I? Ah, *that's* the treacle reset!

'You should learn not to make personal remarks,' Alice said with some severity.

You should learn to make impersonal remarks...

Why? Because individualism is out-of-date, was in 1940 the year *The New World Order* was published. Churchill read

THE PLAGUE DOCTOR

H.G. Wells who writes of 'individualism' in chapter six, the title of it? One moment... *Socialism Unavoidable*.

What is it that the Atlantic world finds most objectionable in the Soviet world of to-day? Is it any disapproval of collectivism as such? Only in the case of a dwindling minority of rich and successful men — and very rarely of the sons of such people. Very few capable men under fifty nowadays remain individualists in political and social matters. They are not even fundamentally anti-Communist. Only it happens that for various reasons the political life of the community is still in the hands of unteachable old-fashioned people. What are called "democracies" suffer greatly from the rule of old men who have not kept pace with the times. The real and effective disapproval, distrust and disbelief in the soundness of the Soviet system lies not in the out-of-date individualism of these elderly types, but in the conviction that it can never achieve efficiency or even maintain its honest ideal of each for all and all for each, unless it has free speech and an insistence upon legally-defined freedoms for the individual within the collectivist framework. We do not deplore the Russian Revolution as a Revolution. We complain that it is not a good enough Revolution and we want a better one.

The more highly things are collectivised the more necessary is a legal system embodying the Rights of Man. This has been forgotten under the Soviets, and so men go in fear there of arbitrary police action. But the more functions your government controls the more need there is for protective law. The objection to Soviet collectivism is that, lacking the antiseptic of legally assured

THE PLAGUE DOCTOR

personal freedom, it will not keep. It professes to be fundamentally a common economic system based on class-war ideas; the industrial director is under the heel of the Party commissar; the political police have got altogether out of hand; and the affairs gravitate inevitably towards an oligarchy or an autocracy protecting its incapacity by the repression of adverse comment.

But these valid criticisms merely indicate the sort of collectivisation that has to be avoided. It does not dispose of collectivism as such. If we in our turn do not wish to be submerged by the wave of Bolshevisation that is evidently advancing from the East, we must implement all these valid objections and create a collectivisation that will be more efficient, more prosperous, tolerant, free and rapidly progressive than the system we condemn. We, who do not like the Stalinised-Marxist state, have, as they used to say in British politics, to "dish" it by going one better. We have to confront Eastern-spirited collectivism with Western-spirited collectivism.

Does the Hatter mean by it, the 'hair collective' has wants, a Mini-coupe, 'drop-head, with the wind in our hair'? Only this spontaneous individual knows which way to go ... His soul does. If you write for a living, even at a continual loss, you have a sense of when you are doing so in contact with God. That being so, the idea of messages being 'channeled' from the inside out, makes sense. An American channel or trance medium, Jane Roberts – her channelings are held at the Yale archives, speaking on behalf of a discarnate entity 'Seth',

THE PLAGUE DOCTOR

confirms that, 'God must love individuals,' he never made anything else. Francis Bacon? He advocates lying to the people in his book *The New Atlantis*. He was locked up in the Tower of London for a short time. Long-winded to a Hare, from Marchester, yes. A fourth industrial revolution, it goes one better: it gives the transhuman false memories for which to punish it, remotely... Emotionally delinquent? Is what you have to be – unresponsive to the Ray of Love - or not to be... FAB I... FABIAN... Who will save this Bacon? Did Bertie Wells, one of Huxley's alumni, hear it verbatim? Did that monkey at Dunmow leave off the fire, brimstone?

Fourteen

Gip not Grip, the name of the son of H.G. Wells by a woman who'd die while Wells is the tenant and regular dinner guest of Frances 'Daisy' Maynard, who'd been so indiscreet about her love life that she was known as 'Babbling Brooke', when she's married to the earl of Warwick. Her estate at Estaines Parva, now Little Easton near Dunmow, was gifted to Henry Maynard by the queen. Her love letters from a young prince are to be bought back from an indebted Daisy by a man who is ennobled for doing so. What's so incriminating about their content other than the obvious, one wonders? Whereas the Liddell sister at Christ Church, her affair with a prince would be terminated on the grounds of her being a commoner, the affair of the prince with Frances Maynard it was encouraged. Queen Victoria, who watches her leave the castle early in her pink riding habit, Daisy's, thinks her 'very fast'. Daisy is a part of the Marlborough social set – this until she is confronted by a newspaper editor with strong social views. He writes what she finds so offensive that she turned up at his office, ready to deal with this social underling. He holds his ground, looks her in the eye, telling her what he thinks of a life led

THE PLAGUE DOCTOR

that has no time for the less fortunate, poor... She counters that he'd no understanding of economics: what she spends in her life of leisure benefits the common man indirectly. She'll leave a changed woman, a convert to his politics with a conscience, social one. She pumps her money into good causes. Women are taught useful skills in a school for them. She offers Little Easton Lodge, her home to the leaders of the new left. She has inherited it under unusual circumstances: she had been taken for a ride by her grandfather who'd decide to leave it, leave everything to her. When the will is read out, butter is thrown at his portrait, pats of it. A champagne socialist the first one, she entertains H.G. Wells and G. Bernard Shaw at Little Easton Lodge, a sprawling pile, that is yet to be burnt down by the pet monkey, who'd overheard Wells at dinner talking of the Morlock in his book about *The Time Machine*. Daisy moves out into an estate cottage where she gardens: she has a 'Shakespeare garden' planted out. She and Shaw raise funds for a National Theatre. He talks of the dark lady of the sonnets. The futurist, Wells, holds forth on the likely direction society will take unless individualism is overcome. Two classes of people – the beautiful Eloi of the Overworld, and the lemur-like Morlocks of the Underworld, survive in a future reached by a dial on Wells' time machine. He dies in 1946; his ideas were and remain immensely influential. The Morlocks, they feed on the Eloi, emerging at night in order to cannibalise on their social betters. Albinos, who can no longer live in the sun, they live in tunnels down a well Wells, his protagonist, explores for himself. Wells is the son of a part-time professional cricketer and a lady's maid at Uppark, where he is allowed to read books from its library. Mary Shelley he acknowledges to have been a strong influence, formative one on him. Was Covid-19 in some part a result of the views expressed over dinner at Daisy's and in his writings by Wells? He'd call himself not an author but journalist, stirring the social pot, cauldron. He is referred to by name in a conversation had between the equerry, Peter Horsley, and the alien, Mr Janus, who tells him, Sir Peter, that he would very much like to meet his employer, the Duke of Edinburgh. So what was it that this monkey, who'd burn the house to the ground, found so offensive in the political theory of a Darwinian, Wells? Did he think monkeys, women, everyone had no spiritual life – no soul – not to guide an individual when the state is unqualified to? Wells was and is playing with fire literally.

Excerpts from 'The Time Machine', Chapter VI onwards:

VI

"'Communism,' said I to myself.

"And on the heels of that came another thought. I looked at the half-dozen little figures that were following me. Then, in a flash, I perceived that all had the same form of costume, the same soft hairless visage, and the same girlish rotundity of limb. It may

THE PLAGUE DOCTOR

seem strange, perhaps, that I had not noticed this before. But everything was so strange. Now, I saw the fact plainly enough. In costume, and in all the differences of texture and bearing that now mark off the sexes from each other, these people of the future were alike. And the children seemed to my eyes to be but the miniatures of their parents. I judged then that the children of that time were extremely precocious, physically at least, and I found afterwards abundant verification of my opinion.

"Seeing the ease and security in which these people were living, I felt that this close resemblance of the sexes was after all what one would expect; for the strength of a man and the softness of a woman, the institution of the family, and the differentiation of occupations are mere militant necessities of an age of physical force. Where population is balanced and abundant, much childbearing becomes an evil rather than a blessing to the State; where violence comes but rarely and offspring are secure, there is less necessity—indeed there is no necessity—for an efficient family, and the specialisation of the sexes with reference to their children's needs disappears. We see some beginnings of this even in our own time, and in this future age it was complete. This, I must remind you, was my speculation at the time. Later, I was to appreciate how far it fell short of the reality.

"While I was musing upon these things, my attention was attracted by a pretty little structure, like a well under a cupola. I thought in a transitory way of the oddness of wells still existing, and then resumed the thread of my speculations. There were no

THE PLAGUE DOCTOR

large buildings towards the top of the hill, and as my walking powers were evidently miraculous, I was presently left alone for the first time. With a strange sense of freedom and adventure I pushed on up to the crest.

"There I found a seat of some yellow metal that I did not recognise, corroded in places with a kind of pinkish rust and half smothered in soft moss, the arm-rests cast and filed into the resemblance of griffins' heads. I sat down on it, and I surveyed the broad view of our old world under the sunset of that long day. It was as sweet and fair a view as I have ever seen. The sun had already gone below the horizon and the west was flaming gold, touched with some horizontal bars of purple and crimson. Below was the valley of the Thames, in which the river lay like a band of burnished steel. I have already spoken of the great palaces dotted about among the variegated greenery, some in ruins and some still occupied. Here and there rose a white or silvery figure in the waste garden of the earth, here and there came the sharp vertical line of some cupola or obelisk. There were no hedges, no signs of proprietary rights, no evidences of agriculture; the whole earth had become a garden.

"So watching, I began to put my interpretation upon the things I had seen, and as it shaped itself to me that evening, my interpretation was something in this way. (Afterwards I found I had got only a half truth—or only a glimpse of one facet of the truth.)

THE PLAGUE DOCTOR

"It seemed to me that I had happened upon humanity upon the wane. The ruddy sunset set me thinking of the sunset of mankind. For the first time I began to realise an odd consequence of the social effort in which we are at present engaged. And yet, come to think, it is a logical consequence enough. Strength is the outcome of need; security sets a premium on feebleness. The work of ameliorating the conditions of life—the true civilising process that makes life more and more secure—had gone steadily on to a climax. One triumph of a united humanity over Nature had followed another. Things that are now mere dreams had become projects deliberately put in hand and carried forward. And the harvest was what I saw!

"After all, the sanitation and the agriculture of today are still in the rudimentary stage. The science of our time has attacked but a little department of the field of human disease, but, even so, it spreads its operations very steadily and persistently. Our agriculture and horticulture destroy a weed just here and there and cultivate perhaps a score or so of wholesome plants, leaving the greater number to fight out a balance as they can. We improve our favourite plants and animals—and how few they are—gradually by selective breeding; now a new and better peach, now a seedless grape, now a sweeter and larger flower, now a more convenient breed of cattle. We improve them gradually, because our ideals are vague and tentative, and our knowledge is very limited; because Nature, too, is shy and slow in our clumsy hands. Some day all this will be better organised, and still better. That is the drift of the current in spite of the eddies. The whole world will be intelligent, educated, and co-operating; things will move faster and faster towards the subjugation of Nature. In the end, wisely and carefully we shall readjust the balance of animal and vegetable life to suit our human needs.

"This adjustment, I say, must have been done, and done well; done indeed for all Time, in the space of Time across which my machine had leapt. The air was free from gnats, the earth from weeds or fungi; everywhere were fruits and sweet and delightful flowers; brilliant butterflies flew hither and thither. The ideal of preventive medicine was attained. Diseases had been stamped out. I saw no evidence of any contagious diseases during all my stay. And I shall have to tell you later that even the processes of putrefaction and decay had been profoundly affected by these changes.

"Social triumphs, too, had been effected...

IX

"It may seem odd to you, but it was two days before I could follow up the new-found clue in what was manifestly the proper way. I felt a peculiar shrinking from those pallid bodies. They were just the half-bleached colour of the worms and things one sees preserved in spirit in a zoological museum. And they were filthily cold to the touch. Probably my shrinking was largely due to the sympathetic influence of the Eloi, whose disgust of the Morlocks I now began to appreciate.

THE PLAGUE DOCTOR

"The next night I did not sleep well. Probably my health was a little disordered. I was oppressed with perplexity and doubt. Once or twice I had a feeling of intense fear for which I could perceive no definite reason. I remember creeping noiselessly into the great hall where the little people were sleeping in the moonlight—that night Weena was among them—and feeling reassured by their presence. It occurred to me even then, that in the course of a few days the moon must pass through its last quarter, and the nights grow dark, when the appearances of these unpleasant creatures from below, these whitened Lemurs, this new vermin that had replaced the old, might be more abundant. And on both these days I had the restless feeling of one who shirks an inevitable duty. I felt assured that the Time Machine was only to be recovered by boldly penetrating these mysteries of underground. Yet I could not face the mystery. If only I had had a companion it would have been different. But I was so horribly alone, and even to clamber down into the darkness of the well appalled me. I don't know if you will understand my feeling, but I never felt quite safe at my back.

"It was this restlessness, this insecurity, perhaps, that drove me farther and farther afield in my exploring expeditions. Going to the south-westward towards the rising country that is now called Combe Wood, I observed far-off, in the direction of nineteenth-century Banstead, a vast green structure, different in character from any I had hitherto seen. It was larger than the largest of the palaces or ruins I knew, and the façade had an Oriental look: the face of it having the lustre, as well as the pale-green

tint, a kind of bluish-green, of a certain type of Chinese porcelain. This difference in aspect suggested a difference in use, and I was minded to push on and explore. But the day was growing late, and I had come upon the sight of the place after a long and tiring circuit; so I resolved to hold over the adventure for the following day, and I returned to the welcome and the caresses of little Weena. But next morning I perceived clearly enough that my curiosity regarding the Palace of Green Porcelain was a piece of self-deception, to enable me to shirk, by another day, an experience I dreaded. I resolved I would make the descent without further waste of time, and started out in the early morning towards a well near the ruins of granite and aluminium.

"Little Weena ran with me. She danced beside me to the well, but when she saw me lean over the mouth and look downward, she seemed strangely disconcerted. 'Good-bye, little Weena,' I said, kissing her; and then putting her down, I began to feel over the parapet for the climbing hooks. Rather hastily, I may as well confess, for I feared my courage might leak away! At first she watched me in amazement. Then she gave a most piteous cry, and running to me, she began to pull at me with her little hands. I think her opposition nerved me rather to proceed. I shook her off, perhaps a little roughly, and in another moment I was in the throat of the well. I saw her agonised face over the parapet, and smiled to reassure her. Then I had to look down at the unstable hooks to which I clung.

THE PLAGUE DOCTOR

"I had to clamber down a shaft of perhaps two hundred yards. The descent was effected by means of metallic bars projecting from the sides of the well, and these being adapted to the needs of a creature much smaller and lighter than myself, I was speedily cramped and fatigued by the descent. And not simply fatigued! One of the bars bent suddenly under my weight, and almost swung me off into the blackness beneath. For a moment I hung by one hand, and after that experience I did not dare to rest again. Though my arms and back were presently acutely painful, I went on clambering down the sheer descent with as quick a motion as possible. Glancing upward, I saw the aperture, a small blue disc, in which a star was visible, while little Weena's head showed as a round black projection. The thudding sound of a machine below grew louder and more oppressive. Everything save that little disc above was profoundly dark, and when I looked up again Weena had disappeared.

"I was in an agony of discomfort. I had some thought of trying to go up the shaft again, and leave the Underworld alone. But even while I turned this over in my mind I continued to descend. At last, with intense relief, I saw dimly coming up, a foot to the right of me, a slender loophole in the wall. Swinging myself in, I found it was the aperture of a narrow horizontal tunnel in which I could lie down and rest. It was not too soon. My arms ached, my back was cramped, and I was trembling with the prolonged terror of a fall. Besides this, the unbroken darkness had had a distressing effect upon my eyes. The air was full of the throb and hum of machinery pumping air down the shaft.

THE PLAGUE DOCTOR

"I do not know how long I lay. I was arroused by a soft hand touching my face. Starting up in the darkness I snatched at my matches and, hastily striking one, I saw three stooping white creatures similar to the one I had seen above ground in the ruin, hastily retreating before the light. Living, as they did, in what appeared to me impenetrable darkness, their eyes were abnormally large and sensitive, just as are the pupils of the abysmal fishes, and they reflected the light in the same way. I have no doubt they could see me in that rayless obscurity, and they did not seem to have any fear of me apart from the light. But, so soon as I struck a match in order to see them, they fled incontinently, vanishing into dark gutters and tunnels, from which their eyes glared at me in the strangest fashion.

"I tried to call to them, but the language they had was apparently different from that of the Overworld people; so that I was needs left to my own unaided efforts, and the thought of flight before exploration was even then in my mind. But I said to myself, 'You are in for it now,' and, feeling my way along the tunnel, I found the noise of machinery grow louder. Presently the walls fell away from me, and I came to a large open space, and striking another match, saw that I had entered a vast arched cavern, which stretched into utter darkness beyond the range of my light. The view I had of it was as much as one could see in the burning of a match.

"Necessarily my memory is vague. Great shapes like big machines rose out of the dimness, and cast grotesque black shadows, in

THE PLAGUE DOCTOR

which dim spectral Morlocks sheltered from the glare. The place, by the bye, was very stuffy and oppressive, and the faint halitus of freshly-shed blood was in the air. Some way down the central vista was a little table of white metal, laid with what seemed a meal. The Morlocks at any rate were carnivorous! Even at the time, I remember wondering what large animal could have survived to furnish the red joint I saw. It was all very indistinct: the heavy smell, the big unmeaning shapes, the obscene figures lurking in the shadows, and only waiting for the darkness to come at me again! Then the match burnt down, and stung my fingers, and fell, a wriggling red spot in the blackness.

X

...Clearly, at some time in the Long-Ago of human decay the Morlocks' food had run short. Possibly they had lived on rats and such-like vermin. Even now man is far less discriminating and exclusive in his food than he was—far less than any monkey. His prejudice against human flesh is no deep-seated instinct. And so these inhuman sons of men——! I tried to look at the thing in a scientific spirit. After all, they were less human and more remote than our cannibal ancestors of three or four thousand years ago. And the intelligence that would have made this state of things a torment had gone. Why should I trouble myself? These Eloi were mere fatted cattle, which the ant-like Morlocks preserved and preyed upon—probably saw to the breeding of. And there was Weena dancing at my side!

THE PLAGUE DOCTOR

"Then I tried to preserve myself from the horror that was coming upon me, by regarding it as a rigorous punishment of human selfishness. Man had been content to live in ease and delight upon the labours of his fellow-man, had taken Necessity as his watchword and excuse, and in the fullness of time Necessity had come home to him. I even tried a Carlyle-like scorn of this wretched aristocracy in decay. But this attitude of mind was impossible. However great their intellectual degradation, the Eloi had kept too much of the human form not to claim my sympathy, and to make me perforce a sharer in their degradation and their Fear.

"I had at that time very vague ideas as to the course I should pursue. My first was to secure some safe place of refuge, and to make myself such arms of metal or stone as I could contrive. That necessity was immediate. In the next place, I hoped to procure some means of fire, so that I should have the weapon of a torch at hand, for nothing, I knew, would be more efficient against these Morlocks. Then I wanted to arrange some contrivance to break open the doors of bronze under the White Sphinx. I had in mind a battering ram. I had a persuasion that if I could enter those doors and carry a blaze of light before me I should discover the Time Machine and escape. I could not imagine the Morlocks were strong enough to move it far away. Weena I had resolved to bring with me to our own time. And turning such schemes over in my mind I pursued our way towards the building which my fancy had chosen as our dwelling.

THE PLAGUE DOCTOR

Had the head of state who told Dr Rima Laibow, 'You know it's almost time for the great culling to begin... The culling of the useless eaters... 90% of the total world population...' has she read him H.G. Wells?

Fifteen

Expert opinion dates the last play in the Shakespearean canon to c.1610... which is the play of *The Tempest* yes.

WILLIAM SHAKESPEARE	1564-1616
FRANCIS BACON	1561-1626
EDWARD DE VERE	1550-1604
HENRY MAYNARD	1547-1610

Susan Maynard? She survives him. Not into the present in a Time Machine no one wonders if she were handed a copy of *The Maze*, Maurice Sandoz's, handed it ahead of time, if she would have pored, puzzled over the names of the main characters in this book illustrated by Dali, again. The fact that she is co-heir of Thomas, 'gentleman-usher of the Star Chamber', does not of itself permit travelling outside of our regular time. So we have *The Maze* being published by Doubleday & Company, Garden City, N.Y., 1946. Yes, same company with which du Maurier, 'she's in love...' Maze, not the cob of maize held in the hand of Henry Maynard on the frontispiece to John Gerrard, his *Herbal*, one 'l' or two. I can

THE PLAGUE DOCTOR

find out little about the man, Henry Maynard, even his date of birth at St Albans, near Hatfield, is something of a mystery. St Albans, C-albani? The relic of St Alban, a bone, is taken home with him by Philip II, to the Palace of the Escorial... Sycorax? Hardly. So what does Edward James of West Dean Park, have a polar bear, purple one, say on his behalf at Port Lligat? Dali is first to go... There was a storm in 1547, a body, incorruptible one on its way from Naples, washed up on the beach, while in the care of a young King Philip. His Spanish shore where Philip shelters his fleet from the storm. Is this why he has this copy of Giorgione's *Tempest* in the hall of his extended house, fisherman's hut at Port Lligat?... More than a conversation piece, it appears – Dali copies it in miniature – in a book on the local witch, Lidia, who had both him and Picasso under her roof at a time when the village was only accessible by donkey... Yes, the fisherman's hut is hers to give the Dalis somewhere to live, 'shelter'. The system of mirrors is something else: Dali's own invention, it allows him to see what is out at sea even when not looking out through a window, from bed. It is not the right book, this one is not to speculate on whether what James had to say about the play, was the catalyst that had Dali him angling his mirrors this way and that to see what? More ivy, not in the water certainly. Sandoz, writing in his White Villa of the White Villa, knew of his island, its unlucky past, ahead of time. He gave the collection of clocks he had built up in his castle, for the public to see on display. The 'pharmaceuticals' fortune he is heir to? No idea, other than a researcher, employee, had

THE PLAGUE DOCTOR

cycled home erratically have discovering LSD. Are we all here?... What was the catalyst of my interest in this, all this. Too mundane, run-of-the-mill to bring into what my publisher requires to be a short paperback, no longer than 128 pages. I'd been online in search of something quite else... and the engine, it thought I would be interested in the four-hundredth anniversary of the bard, so called. Not having been that present at school, the significance of 2016 was lost on me. What was not was the name Miranda in the search engine result, because I could see it was an anagram of an alternative spelling of Maynard. I had Maynards in the family who would have signed any legal document that came their way with a thumb dipped in ink, a thumbprint, yes, for the illiterate man. I knew one thing, though, that Edward de Vere was a candidate in the eyes of leading Shakespearean actors at least, for the bard behind the bard, so why would he leave the name Mainard in his final play, so confusing matters, likely authors... Yes, spelling of surnames, of anything, just about, remains 'fluid' into Tudor times. The discovery of Mark Griffiths, the correspondent at the magazine *Country Life* of the bard on John Gerard's frontispiece, next to William Cecil, on one side or the other of him, depending on whether they are reflected back at us in a public place 'urinal' it'd set me thinking. Neither the Oxfordian nor the believer in Shakespeare found in his features, let alone the cob in his hand, the look of the man they supported for bard. Griffiths sets out on a tour of statues of the great man, actor, until he finds one with an ear,

THE PLAGUE DOCTOR

Shakespeare's, like the one on the frontispiece... Not the effigy of Henry Maynard in his local church, no. He would have involved himself in this significant book's production. Yes, Herbal's... So what do we have or does Sandoz, here in *The Maze*. I am not at all sure. Craven Castle? Cawdor? Macbeth? Son of Beth? The woman remains a virgin all her life. Her double? Hardly... Let me throw some names out.

ELLIE KING
MAJOR POWELL
HARRY SEYMOUR
MARGARET

I have no surname for her, because Sandoz does not give one, no, they are house guests at Craven Castle? Yes – Dali buys a local castle in North Spain, the castle of Pubol, the raven is its symbol, yes emblem. In the film of *The Avengers* or Revengers of Blindheim, John Steed, in the passenger seat of Mrs Peel's E-type Jag, reminds her of her liking for living on the edge, a yew hedge... Red berries? I don't know why, but the maze at Craven is a yew one, *taxus baccata*, too. Where did Dali he meet Sandoz? In Rome, I believe in the thirties, late 1930s. The toad goes for a nocturnal swim in the pond at the centre of the maze. The house guests are told to lock their doors at night [when Toad passes by their rooms in the corridor outside.] Harry Seymour? He's in the room next to narrator Edith's, she'd refer to him as having the look of a Roman imperator. Sir Francis? He is the physician, doctor

THE PLAGUE DOCTOR

whose patient Toad is or was... The narrator? Her first name, Edith that may have something to do with the garden of Eden mentioned at the end in 'The Explanation.'

He [Sir Roger] was master of that element from which life arose. He, again, was the distant ancestor who appeared on earth long before Adam was kneaded out of the dust.

Often, at night, he insisted that we take him to the pond in the maze. There, stripped of his hooded-cloak, his only garment in winter and summer, he threw himself into the water. In his natural element, freed of his dual nature, he became again the distant ancestor of the human race. In winter the ice was broken for him. While we stamped our feet and blew on our fingers, he indulged in extraordinary acrobatics and aquatic feats.

Key to this explanation of him being so long-lived is what is in a chapter in a book that belonged to Craven's owner. The chapter title? It's a long one: 'Of Extraordinary Longevity'... Yes, only one 'e' in evity. Dual nature?

From: 'A Change Occurs at the Castle'.
The eight porters advanced slowly under the heavy load [Toad]. In a gust of wind the torchlight played on the white hair, bent backs, and wrinkled faces of old men. I recognized the old menservants of the castle.

One of the valets at the head of the procession lifted his torch to light up the road. For a moment the light fell on a huge, black, square chest...

THE PLAGUE DOCTOR

Of a toad, his dual nature? It says ...*supported on poles*. Now the narrator has just told Sandoz, her note-taking amanuensis, that her eyes had to become *accustomed* to the low light. So she may be mistaken in what she thinks she sees. If I had not mentioned Hercules shot from behind – the lion in Trafalgar Square is – it would never have occurred to the reader the chest is that of a primate. Edith, her suspicion is aroused earlier on. She is examining what was left behind in the corridor, the morning, by Toad.

It was worth examining more closely. I got down on my knees to see better. A delicate network of fibers showed up, clear cut and graceful. 'It's the impression of a maple or plane-tree leaf.'

The person in the hooded-cloak in Dali's illustration of the 'stone slab?' *There, leaning against a grassy mound...* The woman pointing with her finger at the C of MCTEAM? I've no idea... yes, a comma there is one between *there* and *leaning...* Of Margaret? All we know is what she keeps in her bureau ... *some personal line, four packets of cigarettes, a treatise on the reproduction of eels, and a little paper parcel.* That's about it. The greenish-brown spot? *About the size of the palm of a very large hand.* I'm repeating myself. The carpet it is on, made of. One moment... Rubber, yes, no, it says reproduction of eels, no 'h'.

Sixteen

Speaking of pats of butter, a resident of Coventry reported being chased down the road by a river, lava flow of melted butter from a local processing plant. It was said to be knee-deep with overheated butter on the night of 'Moonlight Sonata' in 1940: the Nazi bombing, flattening of Coventry, from which there came at least a new word, verb in the German language, *coventrieren*. No, no word for Dresden, just a belated twinning of two cities with the one evil tale to tell. The cathedral leant anyway, its tower did, so the operators of machines clearing rubble had to be told to leave it standing. There were those 'modernists', vandals, who were only too happy to see one of Europe's finest medieval cities, Coventry, bombed back to the Stone Age. Ground zero. Children burrowed into walls in their effort to escape the din, the world they found themselves in. Lady Godiva was toppled topless from her plinth. The reincarnation of 'Peeping Tom' aims a well-timed bomb from an open hatch overhead. And there were the indigenous Nazis in Britain, with a soft spot for the fascism of the failed watercolourist Hitler. If someone says 'The Third Way', he may be thought to mean a more recent

THE PLAGUE DOCTOR

government, yet, if one studies the well-researched work, *The Third Way*, by prolific author, Joseph P. Farrell, it seems the Nazis never really went away. Not just paper-clip ones. When individually de-briefed in America, the latter ones admit to having had help of an alien kind with their rapid advances in technology. In his preface to *The Third Way*, Doctor Farrell brings to light a meeting of the Nazi party leadership in August 1944; it was held at a French hotel, the *Maison Rouge* in Strasbourg. German industrialists *agreed to create a worldwide system of front companies, and a system of corporate-Nazi Party liaisons to maintain a covert coordination of Party and corporate interests and goals for postwar Germany and Europe. Careful consideration of the implications of the Hotel* Maison Rouge *meeting indicate that a principal field and center of action for the postwar extraterritorial state that I have called the Nazi International remained centered in Europe.* Farrell moves on to the Madrid Circular of 1953. Is it a blueprint for what is to be a fascist EU? *The Third Way* is in print in 2005. He delays his book on 9/11 until 2016, the date of copyright on the verso title page of:

> *Hidden Finance, Rogue Networks and Secret Sorcery:*
> *The Fascist International, 9/11, and Penetrated Operations.*

The idea of sorcery may strike one as somewhat medieval, older even than Coventry. However, if the Second Ray of Seven is that of Love – Wisdom, then the Seventh Ray has to do with:

THE PLAGUE DOCTOR

7. The Ray of Order or Ceremonial Magic.

The other rays you will find in Alice Bailey's *A Treatise on the Seven Rays*, the publisher: Lucis, formerly Lucifer. Ray Seven 'streaming in' will bring about the fulfilment of Sixth Ray ideals. I'm reading from chapter eight of Robert Graham's *Night Vision: The Powers of Darkness*...

There is a distinction to be made between reputable astrology and astrology that is simplified to the point of misinformation. Reputable astrologers are trained to know the types of energy that influence the planet at any time. These energies radiate from the seven stas of the Great Bear [Ursa Major], and are transmitted to our solar system via related constellations and their ruling planets.

He gives the example of the Fifth Ray [of concrete science or knowledge] *its force being transmitted by the constellations of Aquarius, Sagittarius and Leo.* Nations, too, are on particular Rays, so that Britain, on Ray One, does governance or once did. It was while reading Dr Farrell's take, his 2016 summary of the events of 9/11, that I had a look online inside the 'Emma Booker Elementary School' in Florida, in which President Bush had been reading from 'My Pet Goat' when informed by Presidential Aide Andrew Card of the situation in New York. There was a picture of the front cover of the book *Bear On A Bike* by Stella Blackstone. It had reminded me of the Great Bear or did when I found a bear riding a rocket, with

THE PLAGUE DOCTOR

stars on him, illustrated inside. The hedge on the cover was undulating. I wondered for no good reason if the two wheels of the bike on the front cover were counter-rotating. Then, there was Ari Fleischer, Ariel?, holding up a card saying, 'Don't say anything yet.' I thought it had read like a modernising of Miranda, that speech of hers made to Prospero, asking him to tell who she is, with him concluding, 'Stay, not yet.' There was what I took to be a joke at our expense on the classroom blackboard. It all looked 'staged' to me. Who was the child with the haircut, horns?, over Bush's head. Was he sitting – make that running in for the third rabbit or hare you find in churches? A triskelion. Fleischer, butcher in German? Red meat... painting the town red... Three cards painting the white roses red in the garden of the Queen of Hearts in chapter eight, 'The Queen's Croquet-Ground,' following on from 'A Mad Tea-party'... Who would Emma Booker see in the looking-glass? Who else was in Florida at the Sandpiper Apartments, if not Atta?

PANS PIPER

A toast to a job well done, or *bien cuit* if you work in a family butchery three miles from Lambury. His Driver's License, Atta's? It reads Manhattan? No, Coral Springs in Florida.

SY-CORALICE-NSE... SP-*sonne*...

Coral Springs, in Australia? The location of 'Pine Gap', of the Prospero Supply Station nearby. Act One, scene two.

THE PLAGUE DOCTOR

PROSPERO
>   Dull thing, I say so – he, that Caliban
>   Whom now I keep in service. Thou best know'st
>   What torment I did find thee in. Thy groans
>   Did make wolves howl, and penetrate the breasts
>   Of ever-angry bears. It was a torment
>   To lay upon the damned, which Sycorax
>   Could not again undo. It was mine art,
>   When I arrived and heard thee, that made gape
>   The pine and let thee out.

Made g-ape the pine... The twin towers? Collaspe like pancakes...

PET GOAT, PETER PAN, PAN-S[H]AKES, *CREPES*-SPEER?

Seventeen

H.G. Wells was on the cover, front cover of *Time* magazine on his sixtieth birthday, one day before it to be precise, on September 20th, 1946 [Vol. VIII, No. 12]. A snake is oddly on the cover of *Time* on JANUARY 11, 1999. Across the top right-hand corner, over the letter E of TIME, there is angled to make a triangle with it:

LOTT'S IMPEACHMENT PLAN

LOTT'S is over IMPEACHMENT PLAN. It is as if someone in America – I have only seen it done there – has looped over the corner of a portrait a ribbon, this in order to show the family is in mourning for the sitter... Lott? Not the Biblical Lot with one 't', this Lot has two. The odd thing about it is that in the bottom right-hand corner – I cannot print it out for reasons of safety? Copyright – it reads:

How genetic engineering will change us in the next century Alice into Mabel, Ada? Odd because Lot is in the Book of Genesis, yes. He also, from memory, has sex, incestuous sex with his daughters or he is invited to have it by them.

THE PLAGUE DOCTOR

Along with the account of Tamar and Judah (Genesis 38:11–26), this is one instance of "sperm stealing" in the Bible, in which a woman seduces and has sex with her male relative under false pretences in order to become pregnant. Each case involves a direct ancestor of King David of King David.

Lot's wife is turned to a pillar of salt; she'd looked back at Sodom. Her name? Ado... Edith in some Jewish traditions. I don't doubt that there is a modern Lott with his plan for impeachment... Peach in French? *Peche*, it also means sin, just the accents are changed.

LOTT'S IM SIN MENT PLAN

Plan or plane, borrowing the E of TIME underneath it... On the left of the cover, under the T of TIME, it reads:

SPECIAL
ISSUE
THE
FUTURE
OF
MEDICINE

If the letter W is double U, then the left-hand N of double N or M is covered over by a tree trunk, with no branches, rising from the first I of MEDICINE below. Rather than too obviously looking like the tree in the garden of Eden, with a

THE PLAGUE DOCTOR

snake coiled on it, it could be a variation of the caduceus with one helix of the DNA double-helix turning into a snake as it rises to the left-hand N of double N, M. This snake, it's an S in reverse, reflected in Alice's looking-glass? Reflected anyway.

JANUARY 11, 1999
JANUARY 999111

911? The snake looks to be tasting the air, to be looking at SPECIAL ISSUE... Edith, not Sue... at the CIA? Through CIA at HISSUE? ISSUE... What else? That's about it. You could say the E of THE is over the T of FUTURE, or that this first U of FUTURE makes UFO of OF MEDICINE... The snake it makes a K – a curved one – of the right-hand N of M, that also looks like a half-visible letter A. Add the left-hand N covered over by the top of the tree trunk and you have:

SNAKE

The E being the E in TIME or EMIT... What else?

NE-X-T C-ENT-URY

That's it... If peach is French for sin, what about TIME in French? TEMPS... A pest or plague, one involving a snake? None, the ten plagues of Egypt are listed here.

THE PLAGUE DOCTOR

BLOOD
FROGS
GNATS
FLIES
LIVESTOCK
BOILS
HAIL
LOCUSTS
DARKNESS
FIRSTBORN

No snakes... What about the letters SPECIAL has in common with IMPEACHMENT?

LOTT'S IMPEACHMENT, SPECIAL, SPEACIAL?

Adam was no ape... The W in will? Lower case. Could the snake be looking at apes, not the CIA? See I ape? ADAM is not MACADAM, nor is he an architect called Albert...

OR-MEDICINEXT...

ICI, here in French... I next what? D, 500 to a Roman.

MED I SIN, CINE CENTURY?

Eering not earing... The I of TIME is of course shorter than the trunk of the tree trimmed of its branches...

THE PLAGUE DOCTOR

TIME, TI AE
 IMPEA
TIMEDICINE
TTSIMPEE

I Ten-pest? I snake? Hardly likely, not for a first name.

TIME-SPE[C]T-IME...
LOTT'S
 MENT
  EST
TIMEST, TEMPEST, RED PLAGUE...

Will change us not Sue. It says here, if you were to interweave snake dna with human dna, it would become more resilient to electromagnetic radiation, or more controllable, remotely. So, snake dna and nanotech sensors, they go together. Not hand in leather grove, no, hand in yes snakeskin. Reptilian. Carbon nanotubes of graphene oxide have the same diameter as the microtubules in the brain that process human consciousness. Yes, parallel processing. Synthetic biology, then no biology... Are the thoughts you are thinking, your own, or your soul's? Either would do. Is the incoming stream of consciousness, it you transhuman you? Why ask it? Because Robert Duncan's book *Project: Soul Catcher: Volume Two* it begs the question.

TO BE OR NOT TO BE... HUMAN OR TRANS....

❧ THE PLAGUE DOCTOR ☙

Do what Rudolf Hess didn't. Check your body for scars your past says should be or should not be on it. That's my advice. If the Queen of Hearts threatens you? Cut her head off first.

Eighteen

Did any of it happen? I thought not. I had been in an armchair reading Peter Horsley's autobiography *Sounds From Another Room*. He was in another room in Smith Street, Chelsea, SW3, in conversation with the alien 'Mr Janus.' H.G. Wells his name came up. Mrs Markham – named after Markham Square over the Kings Road from Smith Street – had crossed to my side of it, to a block of flats, to the second floor where Horsley knew to meet her and Janus. The odd thing was that the block was opposite 34 Smith Street, where I lived, down the road from P.L. Travers at number 50. Horsley would go back to the flat a day or so later, to find the sofa Mrs Markham sat on, chair Janus sat on, gone – the flat was unfurnished, he bewildered by a meeting he was in on, had a clear memory of, that – for all he knew – might never have taken place. What would add to his doubt was not having a clear recollection of what the alien has spoken about? No, that was the remarkable thing: Peter Horsley had recorded fourteen pages of what an alien had to say to him, verbatim. And yet, here he admits that he cannot pass common entrance into Winchester; he'd settled for

THE PLAGUE DOCTOR

Wellington instead. Was it his near-death-experience had in a dinghy in which he survived the worst storm in memory, that gave him total recall? And yet, if asked, he cannot recall the physical look of Janus.

It was difficult to describe him with any accuracy; the room was poorly lit by two standard lamps and for most of the time he sat in a deep chair by the side of a not very generous fire. In fact I never really got any physical impression of him.

To add to my doubt as to the veracity of his experience, he has Janus say that aliens like him they don't travel in police and dictator states.

The observers have very highly developed mental powers including extra-sensory, thought reading, hypnosis and the ability to use different dimensions, since all parts of the mind and body have not necessarily evolved in exactly the same fashion. They do not use weapons of any kind and rely solely on their special powers to look after themselves. They make contact only with selected people where secrecy can be maintained. In the loosely-knit societies of the Western world, particularly in England and America, it is fairly easy with the help of friends to do this but not in police and dictator states.

But then I recall, that at the time of Horsley's meeting England was not a police state. There were no Hitlers, no dictators of any hue... We'd won the war after all. Hugh,

❧ THE PLAGUE DOCTOR ❧

Lord Dowding? He is mentioned in the effort, Horsley's, to distance himself from his spiritualism; Horsley is open-minded, yet a sceptic on the whole. That said, he has seen a dead woman walk past him down the aisle of the eight-hundred-year-old church on Thorney Island, near his aerodrome, and been in contact with a dead pilot, and describes how golfer Henry Longhurst told Douglas Bader of the greener greens on the other side – through a fortune-teller. It occurs to me as I write this out, bleary-eyed after waking from a waking dream, a reverie, that it may be that he arranged the meeting with Prince Philip after all but was not at liberty to say so. He would then have had the opportunity to copy down what Janus has to say in a more relaxed manner, just as he says it. Nor did I have a clear impression of the man sitting with his arms crossed across the room from me. If I had seen his hat from the other side, its price in shillings and pence, I may have guessed right at the man beneath it. It was his right cheek I saw only. I could however identify his accent as a Scotsman's, an enlightened one from Edinburgh. He was open to questions, told me as much, so I'd asked him if one can develop mental powers to a degree that 'would cause a politician indigestion?' I told him in a police state one would not hear of it, a proposition like his was. He'd leant over this newspaper, palm over and set it together with a chapter roughed out to be eighteen, both alight. Nei Kung a practitioner of Nei Kung, I'm thinking. He vanishes – like that. He made further contact conditional on it being a conversation about the game of golf, and about

THE PLAGUE DOCTOR

life in Rotterdam, if I've a question for him not to do with the indigestion of sitting MPs. I'm thinking he must have read it, *Adventures in Consciousness*, by Jane Roberts, to do that. Then I woke unwoke. How do I know? I went to the room, where I imagine I'd met him. Not only was he nowhere to be seen, down the back of the chair, his chair, I found the book on golf. The author? A Robert Walker, a Scotsman, long-dead one. It must have been, my mention of a Duncan, that had me mentally conjure him up. The book on golf it had my name in, before I gave it to him. It's impossible. 'Tomorrow and tomorrow and tomorrow,' when we meet next.

Nineteen

The publisher here, with a book on golf from the Reverend Robert Walker, the skater in a portrait by Raeburn. He must have, have conjured it up, the way he did Duncan, King Duncan; all his talk of rays, Henry Raeburn, has led to spontaneous combustion of the contents – chapters eighteen onwards – of this bin, of his wastepaper basket. There's a golf club the wooden shaft of which is missing. The warm palms of Reverend Walker a Nei Kung master?... From what is still legible on the blotting paper on his desk, letters blotted in reverse, he was about to suggest that Dodgson, Lewis Carroll, together with his siblings, all save one of them, got their stammers from the astral plane, where Dickens got his plot and characters from. The blackmailing had begun, therefore, on the other side. Why does he say this? Because if Dodgson's father had had one, a stammer, he'd not have got Croft Rectory, been Archdeacon or Perpetual Curate at Daresbury... Think about it, it is his stammer, his sense of unworthiness for religious work in a church, that leaves Dodgson, Lewis Carroll, on the outside of vocational life. I have found it, not a medal, no a book down the back of his

THE PLAGUE DOCTOR

seat, on what it is to be Dutch, to be from Rotterdam, to skate by the full moonlight. If the dam it fails? There would be nothing left to find, no no guide book by Walker on how to skate it the Dutch way. Chapter one on 'Seeing your Shadow grow below the Ice at Night...' A long one. Try the bathroom? No Archimedes in a tepid bath, deep thought. No Eureka moment ...no weighing of one's shadow no. This may be something, 'Notes for Ch. 19,' chapter 19, then. He composes, Carroll does, the variation of the song, Ariel's sung in Ferdinand's ear in mourning for King Alonso – a variation to do with the belfry, in 1873, the very year he visits speech therapist 'Rivers', a skater, nocturnal one himself. Not on the thin ice of the River Isis but with a Miss Flite ... And Carroll tells Rivers he cannot pronounce the letter 'c' in public, in a shop, schop? So this would have been the proof that he Carroll was looking for, to confirm that the 'c' is unseen in the play of *The Tempest*. Six impossible things, before breakfast? '...my difficulties with "p" in such combinations as "impossible"' leaves him with no hope? Rather frustrated that 'the hope I had formed of being very soon able to help in church again,' it's one more once more dashed.

Christ Church, Oxford
19 December, 1873

My dear Rivers,
   ... Just now I am in a bad way for speaking, and a good deal discouraged. I actually so entirely broke down, twice lately, over a hard 'C', that I had to spell the word! Once was in a shop, which

THE PLAGUE DOCTOR

made it more annoying; however it is an annoyance one must make up one's mind to bear, I suppose, now and then – especially when, as now, I have been rather hard worked...
Very truly yours,
C.L. Dodgson

Entirely? No 'y'. We are not back at Abbots three miles from Lambury mourning the demise of the Miherin man. Then on December 27, 1873, this, from The Chestnuts, Guildford where he moved his sisters after the Archdeacon's sudden death.

My dear Rivers,
  ... Thanks for advice about hard 'C', which I acknowledge to be my vanquisher in single-hand combat, at the present. As to working the jaw more, your advice is within my power, generally: but as to the direction to 'keep the back of the tongue down,' in the moment of difficulty, I fear you might almost as well advise me to stand on my head! Believe me.
Very truly yours,
C.L. Dodgson

Believe me, three syllables or two. Belfry? Was he the Reverend Robert Walker known to him, Carroll too? Three tomorrows. If there is more that passes between him author and Reverend Walker, we'll have it bound in leather do so for posterity. One would think a mathematics don he'd be up for it, to count to ten, if others they fall short. No files down a

THE PLAGUE DOCTOR

seat nor reproduced eels no, that treatise? It is one for him, Malise. We are all out of blotting paper just marginalia left, to do with the play, code, no talk of aliens. His self-portrait, Carroll's? A third eye, not die. Dr Laibow she misheard her the head of state. The marginalia can wait, it will have to. No EU.

Twenty

By a process of elimination, subtraction, we have identified the book missing from the author's shelf, his study yes. We have accounted for every book in the select bibliography of the book *The Bee Order*, all except one, which is *Slaves Of Isis*. I have it a new copy of this book open in front of me... No, no mention of a tea-party, mad one on the River Isis that I can see. No mention of a medieval 'healing well' called a treacle well at the church, Binsey's, where the picnic took place in 1862. There is in the dedication what looks to be a reference to the shadows you find in paintings, if they do not themselves throw shadows

> *I dedicate Slaves Of Isis to those of my readers who so religiously polish and in this way give earthly life to the shadows of the dark recesses of their minds. May you be led forward by the black shine of these illumined silhouettes, and by the sound of their booted tread be soon guided into the presence and service of the Divine.*

THE PLAGUE DOCTOR

Madame de Morville? Yes... The Hydra? There is a possible mention of one in this book *That Hideous Strength* which has for an opening quote:

> 'The Shadow of that hyddeous strength
> Sax myle and more it is of length.'

The colour of the laces in the author's shoes? They are neither red or black... nor any other colour, no, they look like shoes that are shed in order to be replaced by a new pair. High heels worn down over time... or by a file. What was it that the Reverend Walker and the 'femme fatale', they had in common? I can only think that the rasping sound of file on stiletto to a snowblind man, it would sound like a fellow skater on ice or below it, yes. Had he, Malise, another book in mind 'when he went up in smoke?' Up or down... It is not clear from the blotting paper if these are marks made by a raven's beak, made randomly, or intended as punctuation marks. Reading between the lines and at the drop of a hat, without giving it much thought, I'd say he was planning a book on the effect on the health of the young Dickens's who are pecked on the ankles by the pet raven. Was this the transformation that Reverend Walker in gathering speed, had hoped for, to take off, do so like Mr Poe? Could the rasping, filing be the cause of the fire, 'like two sticks rubbed together?' Or was it the sight of a character from the book he was reading that has him combust, vanish into space? Mr Poe would pretend to be one, to fly like a raven. Was he taking down dictation from a bird question mark

Marginalia

MR GRIDLEY, LEEK, B-LEAK HOUSE
SIR LEICESTER DEDLOCK, WEDLOCK
SMALLW[H]EED[LE] = MISS GRIDLEY [SMALLWEEDLEY?]
SIR LEICESTER DEDLOCK, DEDLEY, L to R, REY?
LOCK, *LE VERROU*, *LA ESCLUSA*, *LLAVE*, LAVINIA?
MRS PARDIGGLE, LEOPARD GRIDLE, GIRDLE?
HO-NO-RIA BARBARY, BARNABY G-RUDGE, *RENCOR*...
BARBARY COAST, SPANISH APE? WITCH, 1542?
ROBERT DUDLEY, EARL OF LEICESTER...
 JUDY SMALLWEED grandaughter...
BARBABY, CAPTAIN J'AIME WHORE-HAW *DON*, AMY...
DEDLOCK, ROCKINGHAM CASTLE, TULKINGHORN?
RICHARD [CARSTONE] and L to RAVINIA WAT-SON?
MARNDYCE V MARNDYCE = ESTHER SUMMERSON...
ALLAN WOODCOURT = ESTHER SUMMERSON
ADA CLARE, *CLE*, RICHARD CARSTONE, CASTOR OIL...
MR KROOK, MRS ROOK? JELLIBABY? GIN...
ARTHUR GRIDE, NICHOLAS NICKLEBY...
MISS LA CREEVY, MISS SNEVELLICCI?
MR BAYHAM BADGER... BLAIREAU?
5G TOWELLS, HYDRA VULGARIS?
TRANSHUMANISM, HIPNOSIS?

THE PLAGUE DOCTOR

JANE ROBERTS, 'SETH' on HYPNOSIS:

Space travel, in your terms, will develop in a seemingly extravagant and startling fashion, only to be dumped as such when your scientists discover that space as you know it is a distortion, and that journeying from one so-called galaxy to another is done by divesting the physical body from camouflage. The vehicle of so-called space travel is mental and psychic mobility, in terms of psychic transformation of energy, enabling spontaneous and instantaneous mobility through the spacious present ... As to the means, the very simplest and crudest but still to be adopted method will prove to be hypnosis, simply because at this point your personalities cannot trust their own abilities but must rely upon suggestion from the outside.

– From session 45, April 20, 1964

Appendix [1]

THE RAVEN

Once upon a midnight dreary, while I pondered, weak and weary,
Over many a quaint and curious volume of forgotten lore—
While I nodded, nearly napping, suddenly there came a tapping,
As of some one gently rapping, rapping at my chamber door.
"'Tis some visitor," I muttered, "tapping at my chamber door—
    Only this and nothing more."

Ah, distinctly I remember it was in the bleak December;
And each separate dying ember wrought its ghost upon the floor.
Eagerly I wished the morrow;—vainly I had sought to borrow
From my books surcease of sorrow—sorrow for the lost Lenore—
For the rare and radiant maiden whom the angels name Lenore—
    Nameless here for evermore.

And the silken, sad, uncertain rustling of each purple curtain
Thrilled me—filled me with fantastic terrors never felt before;
So that now, to still the beating of my heart, I stood repeating
"'Tis some visitor entreating entrance at my chamber door—
Some late visitor entreating entrance at my chamber door;—
    This it is and nothing more."

THE PLAGUE DOCTOR

Presently my soul grew stronger; hesitating then no longer,
"Sir," said I, "or Madam, truly your forgiveness I implore;
But the fact is I was napping, and so gently you came rapping,
And so faintly you came tapping, tapping at my chamber door,
That I scarce was sure I heard you"—here I opened wide the
    door;—
  Darkness there and nothing more.

Deep into that darkness peering, long I stood there wondering,
    fearing,
Doubting, dreaming dreams no mortal ever dared to dream before;
But the silence was unbroken, and the stillness gave no token,
And the only word there spoken was the whispered word, "Lenore?"
This I whispered, and an echo murmured back the word,
    "Lenore!"—
  Merely this and nothing more.

Back into the chamber turning, all my soul within me burning,
Soon again I heard a tapping somewhat louder than before.
"Surely," said I, "surely that is something at my window lattice;
Let me see, then, what thereat is, and this mystery explore—
Let my heart be still a moment and this mystery explore;—
  'Tis the wind and nothing more!"

Open here I flung the shutter, when, with many a flirt and flutter,
In there stepped a stately Raven of the saintly days of yore;
Not the least obeisance made he; not a minute stopped or stayed he;
But, with mien of lord or lady, perched above my chamber door—

THE PLAGUE DOCTOR

Perched upon a bust of Pallas just above my chamber door—
   Perched, and sat, and nothing more.

Then this ebony bird beguiling my sad fancy into smiling,
By the grave and stern decorum of the countenance it wore,
"Though thy crest be shorn and shaven, thou," I said, "art sure no craven,
Ghastly grim and ancient Raven wandering from the Nightly shore—
Tell me what thy lordly name is on the Night's Plutonian shore!"
   Quoth the Raven "Nevermore."

Much I marvelled this ungainly fowl to hear discourse so plainly,
Though its answer little meaning—little relevancy bore;
For we cannot help agreeing that no living human being
Ever yet was blessed with seeing bird above his chamber door—
Bird or beast upon the sculptured bust above his chamber door,
   With such name as "Nevermore."

But the Raven, sitting lonely on the placid bust, spoke only
That one word, as if his soul in that one word he did outpour.
Nothing farther then he uttered—not a feather then he fluttered—
Till I scarcely more than muttered "Other friends have flown before—
On the morrow he will leave me, as my Hopes have flown before."
   Then the bird said "Nevermore."

THE PLAGUE DOCTOR

Startled at the stillness broken by reply so aptly spoken,
"Doubtless," said I, "what it utters is its only stock and store
Caught from some unhappy master whom unmerciful Disaster
Followed fast and followed faster till his songs one burden bore —
Till the dirges of his Hope that melancholy burden bore
  Of 'Never — nevermore'."

But the Raven still beguiling all my fancy into smiling,
Straight I wheeled a cushioned seat in front of bird, and bust
    and door;
Then, upon the velvet sinking, I betook myself to linking
Fancy unto fancy, thinking what this ominous bird of yore —
What this grim, ungainly, ghastly, gaunt, and ominous bird
    of yore
  Meant in croaking "Nevermore."

This I sat engaged in guessing, but no syllable expressing
To the fowl whose fiery eyes now burned into my bosom's core;
This and more I sat divining, with my head at ease reclining
On the cushion's velvet lining that the lamp-light gloated o'er,
But whose velvet-violet lining with the lamp-light gloating o'er,
  She shall press, ah, nevermore!

Then, methought, the air grew denser, perfumed from an unseen
    censer
Swung by Seraphim whose foot-falls tinkled on the tufted floor.
"Wretch," I cried, "thy God hath lent thee — by these angels he hath
    sent thee

THE PLAGUE DOCTOR

Respite—respite and nepenthe from thy memories of Lenore;
Quaff, oh quaff this kind nepenthe and forget this lost Lenore!"
    Quoth the Raven "Nevermore."

"Prophet!" said I, "thing of evil!—prophet still, if bird or devil!—
Whether Tempter sent, or whether tempest tossed thee here ashore,
Desolate yet all undaunted, on this desert land enchanted—
On this home by Horror haunted—tell me truly, I implore—
Is there—is there balm in Gilead?—tell me—tell me, I implore!"
    Quoth the Raven "Nevermore."

"Prophet!" said I, "thing of evil!—prophet still, if bird or devil!
By that Heaven that bends above us—by that God we both adore—
Tell this soul with sorrow laden if, within the distant Aidenn,
It shall clasp a sainted maiden whom the angels name Lenore—
Clasp a rare and radiant maiden whom the angels name Lenore."
    Quoth the Raven "Nevermore."

"Be that word our sign of parting, bird or fiend!" I shrieked,
    upstarting—
"Get thee back into the tempest and the Night's Plutonian shore!
Leave no black plume as a token of that lie thy soul hath spoken!
Leave my loneliness unbroken!—quit the bust above my door!
Take thy beak from out my heart, and take thy form from off
    my door!"
    Quoth the Raven "Nevermore."

THE PLAGUE DOCTOR

And the Raven, never flitting, still is sitting, still is sitting
On the pallid bust of Pallas just above my chamber door;
And his eyes have all the seeming of a demon's that is dreaming,
And the lamp-light o'er him streaming throws his shadow on
   the floor;
And my soul from out that shadow that lies floating on the floor
  Shall be lifted—nevermore!

Appendix [2]

LENORE

Ah broken is the golden bowl! the spirit flown forever!
Let the bell toll!—a saintly soul floats on the Stygian river;
And, Guy De Vere, hast thou no tear?—weep now or never more!
See! on yon drear and rigid bier low lies thy love, Lenore!
Come! let the burial rite be read—the funeral song be sung!—
An anthem for the queenliest dead that ever died so young—
A dirge for her the doubly dead in that she died so young.

"*Wretches! ye loved her for her wealth and hated her for her pride,*
"*And when she fell in feeble health, ye blessed her—that she died!*
"*How shall the ritual, then, be read?—the requiem how be sung*
"*By you—by yours, the evil eye,—by yours, the slanderous tongue*
"*That did to death the innocent that died, and died so young?*"

Peccavimus; but rave not thus! and let a Sabbath song
Go up to God so solemnly the dead may feel so wrong!
The sweet Lenore hath "gone before," with Hope, that flew beside
Leaving thee wild for the dear child that should have been thy
    bride—
For her, the fair and debonair, that now so lowly lies,
The life upon her yellow hair but not within her eyes—
The life still there, upon her hair—the death upon her eyes.

◈§ THE PLAGUE DOCTOR §◈

"Avaunt! to-night my heart is light. No dirge will I upraise,
"But waft the angel on her flight with a Pæan of old days!
"Let no bell toll! — lest her sweet soul, amid its hallowed mirth,
"Should catch the note, as it doth float up from the damnéd Earth.
"To friends above, from fiends below, the indignant ghost is riven —
"From Hell unto a high estate far up within the Heaven —
"From grief and groan, to a golden throne, beside the King of Heaven."

Select Bibliography

Morville, Madame de, *Slaves of Isis* [Stiletto Books, 2000, ISBN 0-9525463-6-1].

Morville, Madame de, *The Chateau* [Stiletto Books, 2001, ISBN 0-9525463-3-7].

Morville, Madame de, *Temple of Isis* [Stiletto Books, 2001, ISBN 0-9525463-2-9].

Morville, Madame de, *The Priestess* [Stiletto Books, 2002, ISBN 1-903908-06-X].

Morville, Madame de, *Heel! The New World Order* [Stiletto Books, 2002, ISBN 1-903908-05-1].

Morville, Madame de, *The Venetian Night* [Stiletto Books, 2002, ISBN 1-903908-08-6].

Morville, Madame de, *The Snow Leopard* [Stiletto Books, 2002, ISBN 1-903908-00-0].

Morville, Madame de, *The Chameleon Tongue* [Stiletto Books, 2002, ISBN 1-903908-01-9].

Morville, Madame de, *Hall of Mirrors* [Stiletto Books, 2003, ISBN 1-903908-04-3].

Morville, Madame de, *The Scorpion Boot* [Stiletto Books, 2003, ISBN 1-903908-07-8].

Morville, Madame de, *Hall of Judgement* [Stiletto Books, 2003, ISBN 1-903908-09-4].

Morville, Madame de, *The Ascension* [Stiletto Books, 2004, ISBN 1–903908–10–8].

Morville, Madame de, *The Winter Queen* [Stiletto Books, 2004, ISBN 1–903908–26–4].

Morville, Madame de, *Paradise Lost* [Stiletto Books, 2004, ISBN 1–903908–27–2].

Morville, Madame de, *Amazon in Bronze* [Stiletto Books, 2004, ISBN 1–903908–30–2].

Morville, Madame de, *The Argonaut* [Stiletto Books, 2004, ISBN 1–903908–32–9].

Morville, Madame de, *The Forbidden Fruit* [Stiletto Books, 2004, ISBN 1–903908–33–7].

Morville, Madame de, *The Gates of Horn* [Stiletto Books, 2005, ISBN 1–903908–36–1].

Morville, Madame de, *The Mausoleum* [Stiletto Books, 2005, ISBN 1–903908–40–X].

Morville, Madame de, *The Gates of Ivory* [Stiletto Books, 2005, ISBN 1–903908–42–6].

Morville, Madame de, *Book of the Dead* [Stiletto Books, 2005, ISBN 1–903908–43–4].

Morville, Madame de, *The Neophyte* [Stiletto Books, 2006, ISBN 1–903908–45–0].

Morville, Madame de, *Etiquette* [Stiletto Books, 2006, ISBN 978–1–903908–46–4].

Morville, Madame de, *The Cardinal Sin* [Stiletto Books, 2008, ISBN 978–1–903908–49–5].

Morville, Madame de, *The Minotaur* [Stiletto Books, 2009, ISBN 978–1–903908–42–6].

Morville, Madame de, *The Labyrinth* [Stiletto Books, 2010, ISBN 978–1–903908–44–0].
Morville, Madame de, *The Amphibian* [Stiletto Books, 2010, ISBN 978–1–903908–50–1].
Morville, Madame de, *The Metamorphosis* [Stiletto Books, 2011, ISBN 978–1–903908–51–8].
Morville, Madame de, *The Bridge of Sighs* [Stiletto Books, 2012, ISBN 978-1-903908-80-8].
Morville, Madame de, *The Nocturnal Visitor* [Stiletto Books, 2014, ISBN 978-1-903908-57-0].
Morville, Madame de, *The Eye of a Needle* [Stiletto Books, 2014, ISBN 978-1-903908-64-8].
Morville, Madame de, *The Troubadour* [Stiletto Books, 2015, ISBN 978-1-903908-99-0].
Morville, Madame de, *Pandora's Boots* [Stiletto Books, 2016, ISBN 978-1-903908-96-9].
Morville, Madame de, *Daydreams of Leather* [Stiletto Books, 2016, ISBN 978-1-903908-94-5].
Morville, Madame de, *Portrait of a Fantast* [Stiletto Books, 2016, ISBN 978-1-903908-84-6].
Morville, Madame de, *The Stalagmite Men* [Stiletto Books, 2016, ISBN 978-1-903908-71-6].
Morville, Madame de, *Insect Karma* [Stiletto Books, 2017, ISBN 978-1-903908-75-4].
Morville, Madame de, *Valley of the Queens* [Stiletto Books, 2017, ISBN 978-1-903908-90-7].
Morville, Madame de, *The Mannequin's Dream* [Stiletto Books, 2017, ISBN 978-1-903908-69-3].

THE PLAGUE DOCTOR

Morville, Madame de, *The Prodigal Slave* [Stiletto Books, 2017, ISBN 978-1-903908-82-2].

Morville, Madame de, *The Pygmalion Man* [Stiletto Books, 2017, ISBN 978-1-903908-54-9].

Morville, Madame de, *The Schizophrenic Boot* [Stiletto Books, 2017, ISBN 978-1-903908-62-4].

Morville, Madame de, *The Riding Habit* [Stiletto Books, 2017, ISBN 978-1-903908-98-3].

Morville, Madame de, *Renaissance Woman* [Stiletto Books, 2018, ISBN 978-1-903908-77-8].

Morville, Madame de, *The Icequeen's Shadow* [Stiletto Books, 2018, ISBN 978-1-903908-61-7].

Morville, Madame de, *First Impressions* [Stiletto Books, 2018, ISBN 978-1-903908-56-3].

Morville, Madame de, *The Human Parrot* [Stiletto Books, 2018, ISBN 978-1-903908-58-7].

Morville, Madame de, *The Tightrope Walker* [Stiletto Books, 2018, ISBN 978-1-903908-74-7].

Morville, Madame de, *The Practical Joker* [Stiletto Books, 2018, ISBN 978-1-903908-36-5].

Morville, Madame de, *The Nightwatchman* [Stiletto Books, 2018, ISBN 978-1-903908-67-9].

Morville, Madame de, *The Double Agent* [Stiletto Books, 2018, ISBN: 978-1-903908-53-2].

Morville, Madame de, *Lady of the Night* [Stiletto Books, 2018, ISBN: 978-1-903908-95-2].

Morville, Madame de, *Lady of the Lake* [Stiletto Books, 2019, ISBN: 978-1-903908-85-3].

Morville, Madame de, *The Book of Hours* [Stiletto Books, 2019, ISBN: 978-1-903908-34-1].

Morville, Madame de, *The Fall of Pisa* [Stiletto Books, 2019, ISBN: 978-1-903908-40-2].

Morville, Madame de, *The Understudy* [Stiletto Books, 2019, ISBN: 978-1-903908-87-7].

Morville, Madame de, *The False Prophet* [Stiletto Books, 2019, ISBN: 978-1-903908-31-0].

Morville, Madame de, *The Truffle-hunter* [Stiletto Books, 2019, ISBN: 978-1-903908-24-2].

Morville, Madame de, *The Pearl Diver* [Stiletto Books, 2019, ISBN: 978-1-903908-27-3].

Morville, Madame de, *The Hourglass Figure* [Stiletto Books, 2019, ISBN: 978-1-903908-81-5].

Morville, Madame de, *The Mothwoman* [Stiletto Books, 2019, ISBN: 978-1-903908-92-1].

Morville, Madame de, *The Dance of Death* [Stiletto Books, 2019, ISBN: 978-1-903908-91-4].

Morville, Madame de, *The Sarcophagus* [Stiletto Books, 2019, ISBN: 978-1-903908-83-9].

Morville, Madame de, *The Phoenix* [Stiletto Books, 2019, ISBN: 978-1-903908-65-5].

Morville, Madame de, *The Philatelist* [Stiletto Books, 2019, ISBN: 978-1-903908-52-5].

Morville, Madame de, *The Somnambulist* [Stiletto Books, 2020, ISBN: 978-1-903908-70-9].

Morville, Madame de, *A Modern Nefertiti* [Stiletto Books, 2020, ISBN: 978-1-903908-89-1].

THE PLAGUE DOCTOR

Morville, Madame de, *The Samaritan* [Stiletto Books, 2020, ISBN: 978-1-903908-79-2].

Morville, Madame de, *The Fallen Angel* [Stiletto Books, 2020, ISBN 978-1-903908-78-5].

Morville, Madame de, *The Tower of Babel* [Stiletto Books, 2020, ISBN: 978-1-903908-76-1].

Morville, Madame de, *The Usherette* [Stiletto Books, 2020, ISBN: 978-1-903908-55-6].

Morville, Madame de, *The Rendezvous* [Stiletto Books, 2020, ISBN: 978-1-903908-63-1].

Morville, Madame de, *The Boutique* [Stiletto Books, 2020, ISBN: 978-1-903908-72-3].

Morville, Madame de, *The Pipistrelle* [Stiletto Books, 2020, ISBN: 978-1-903908-59-4].

Morville, Madame de, *The Plagiarist* [Stiletto Books, 2020, ISBN: 978-1-903908-66-2].

Morville, Madame de, *The Third Eye* [Stiletto Books, 2020, ISBN: 978-1-8383591-3-3].

Morville, Madame de, *Memento Mori* [Stiletto Books, 2021, ISBN: 978-1-8383591-8-8].

Morville, Madame de, *The Grimoire* [Stiletto Books, 2021, ISBN: 978-1-8383591-7-1].

Morville, Madame de, *The Phantom* [Stiletto Books, 2021, ISBN: 978-1-8383591-9-5].

Morville, Madame de, *The Clairvoyant* [Stiletto Books, 2021, ISBN: 978-1-8383591-4-0].

Morville, Madame de, *The Prelate Scryer* [Stiletto Books, 2021, ISBN: 978-1-8383591-5-7].

Morville, Madame de, *The Telepath* [Stiletto Books, 2021, ISBN: 978-1-8383591-0-2].

Morville, Madame de, *The Succubus* [Stiletto Books, 2021, ISBN: 978-1-8383591-1-9].

Morville, Madame de, *The Vampyre* [Stiletto Books, 2021, ISBN: 978-1-8383591-6-4].

Morville, Madame de, *The Primate Eye* [Stiletto Books, 2022, ISBN: 978-1-8383591-2-6].

Morville, Madame de, *The Remorse Code* [Stiletto Books, 2022, ISBN: 978-1-7397802-1-0].

Morville, Madame de, *The Typing Pool* [Stiletto Books, 2022, ISBN: 978-1-7397802-0-3].

Morville, Madame de, *The Taxidermist* [Stiletto Books, 2022, ISBN: 978-1-7397802-2-7].

Morville, Madame de, *The Rocking Horse* [Stiletto Books, 2022, ISBN: 978-1-7397802-3-4].

Maynard, G.M.B., *The Moving Finger* [Stiletto Books, 2022, ISBN: 978-1-7397802-4-1].

Maynard, G.M.B., *Noctambule: Volume One* [Stiletto Books, 2022, ISBN: 978-1-7397802-5-8].

Maynard, G.M.B., *Persephone: Volume One* [Stiletto Books, 2022, ISBN: 978-1-7397802-6-5].

Maynard, G.M.B., *Left Eye, Right* [Stiletto Books, 2022, ISBN: 978-1-7397802-7-2].

Maynard, G.M.B., *The Pyramid Eye* [Stiletto Books, 2022, ISBN: 978-1-7397802-8-9].

Maynard, G.M.B., *The Angel of Death* [Stiletto Books, 2022, ISBN: 978-1-7397802-9-6].

THE PLAGUE DOCTOR

Maynard, G.M.B., *The Siren* [Stiletto Books, 2022, ISBN: 978-1-7391764-0-2].

Maynard, G.M.B., *The Botanist* [Stiletto Books, 2022, ISBN: 978-1-7391764-8-8].

Maynard, G.M.B., *Left Bite, Right* [Stiletto Books, 2023, ISBN: 978-1-7391764-1-9].

Maynard, G.M.B., *The Globe Itself* [Stiletto Books, 2023, ISBN: 978-1-7391764-4-0].

M. Boutflower, *The Gibbet Tree* [Stiletto Books, 2023, ISBN: 978-1-7391764-6-4].

M. Boutflower, *The Double Man* [Stiletto Books, 2023, ISBN: 978-1-7391764-9-5].

M. Boutflower, *An Idle Theme: Volume One* [Stiletto Books, 2023, ISBN: 978-1-7391764-3-3].

M. Boutflower, *An Idle Theme: Volume Two* [Stiletto Books, 2023, ISBN: 978-1-7391764-7-1].

M. Boutflower, *An Idle Theme: Volume Three* [Stiletto Books, 2023, ISBN: 978-1-7391764-2-6].

M. Boutflower, *Circe's Lover: Volume One* [Stiletto Books, 2023, ISBN: 978-1-7391764-5-7].

M. Boutflower, *Circe's Lover: Volume Two* [Stiletto Books, 2023, ISBN: 978-1-7395119-9-9].

M. Boutflower, *The Relic Bone* [Stiletto Books, 2023, ISBN: 978-1-7395119-2-0].

M. Boutflower, *The Hydra of Lerna* [Stiletto Books, 2023, ISBN: 978-1-7395119-4-4].

Maynard, G.M.B., *The Sylph* [Stiletto Books, 2023, ISBN: 978-1-7395119-3-7].

M. Boutflower, *The Death of a Vampyre* [Stiletto Books, 2023, ISBN: 978-1-7395119-0-6].

M. Boutflower, *The Kiss of Death* [Stiletto Books, 2024, ISBN: 978-1-7395119-5-1].

M. Boutflower, *The Masque* [Stiletto Books, 2024, ISBN: 978-1-7395119-7-5].

M. Boutflower, *The Crow's Nest* [Stiletto Books, 2024, ISBN: 978-1-7395119-6-8].

M. Boutflower, *The Trade Secret* [Stiletto Books, 2024, ISBN: 978-1-7395119-1-3].

M. Boutflower, *Female Ivy* [Stiletto Books, 2024, ISBN: 978-1-7385787-0-2].

M. Boutflower, *Fallen Gods* [Stiletto Books, 2024, ISBN: 978-1-7385787-1-9].

M. Boutflower, *The Lidless Eye* [Stiletto Books, 2024, ISBN: 978-1-7385787-8-8].

M. Boutflower, *Memento Mori* [Stiletto Books, 2024, ISBN: 978-1-7385787-4-0].

M. Boutflower, *The Recidivist* [Stiletto Books, 2024, ISBN: 978-1-7385787-9-5].

M. Boutflower, *The Muse* [Stiletto Books, 2024, ISBN: 978-1-7385787-3-3].

M. Boutflower, *The Garden of Eden* [Stiletto Books, 2024, ISBN: 978-1-7385787-7-1].

M. Boutflower, *The Cardinal Sin* [Stiletto Books, 2024, ISBN: 978-1-7385787-6-4].

M. Boutflower, *The Accomplice* [Stiletto Books, 2024, ISBN: 978-1-7385787-5-7].

THE PLAGUE DOCTOR

M. Boutflower, *The Lidded Eye* [Stiletto Books, 2024, ISBN: 978-1-7385787-2-6].
M. Boutflower, *Glass Eyes* [Stiletto Books, 2024, ISBN: 978-1-0683381-9-9].
M. Boutflower, *Blood Ties* [Stiletto Books, 2024, ISBN: 978-1-0683381-4-4].
M. Boutflower, *Death Throes* [Stiletto Books, 2025, ISBN: 978-1-0683381-0-6].
M. Boutflower, *The Styx* [Stiletto Books, 2025, ISBN: 978-1-0683381-2-0].
M. Boutflower, *The Bee Order* [Stiletto Books, 2025, ISBN: 978-1-0683381-8-2].
Graham, Robert, *Night Vision: The Powers of Darkness* [Matrix, 2000, ISBN 978-1-903908-23-5].
Graham, Robert, *Night Vision: The Powers of Darkness* [Matrix, 2017, ISBN 978-1-903908-68-6, 2nd edition].
Maynard, G.M.B., *Prospero's Daugher* [Matrix, 2015, ISBN 978-1-903908-97-6].
Maynard, G.M.B., *Hidden Faces* [Matrix, 2018, ISBN 978-1-903908-30-3].

Printed in Dunstable, United Kingdom